complete

indian

complete
indian

hamlyn

U.K. edition first published in 1998
by Hamlyn
2–4 Heron Quays
London E14 4JP

Distributed in the United States and Canada by
Sterling Publishing Co., Inc.
387 Park Avenue South
New York, NY 10016

ISBN 0 600 599 477

Printed in China

NOTES

Eggs should be medium to large unless otherwise stated.
The USDA advises that eggs should not be consumed raw. This
book contains dishes made with raw or lightly cooked eggs. It is
advisable for more vulnerable people such as pregnant and nursing
mothers, invalids, the elderly, babies, and young children to avoid
uncooked or lightly cooked dishes made with eggs. Once
prepared, these dishes should be kept refrigerated and used
promptly.

Meat and poultry should be cooked thoroughly. To test if poultry
is cooked, pierce the flesh through the thickest part with a skewer
or fork—the juices should run clear, never pink or red. Do not re-
freeze poultry that has been frozen previously and thawed.
Do not re-freeze a cooked dish that has been frozen previously.

Milk should be whole milk unless otherwise stated.

Nut and Nut Derivatives
This book includes dishes made with nuts and nut derivatives. It
is advisable for those with known allergic reactions to nuts and
nut derivatives and those who may be potentially vulnerable to
these allergies, such as pregnant and nursing mothers, invalids,
the elderly, babies, and children to avoid dishes made with nuts
and nut oils. It is also wise to check the labels of pre-prepared
ingredients for the possible inclusion of nut derivatives.

Pepper should be freshly ground black pepper unless otherwise
stated.

Fresh herbs should be used, unless otherwise stated. If
unavailable, use dried herbs as an alternative, but halve the
quantities stated.

Ovens should be pre-heated to the specified temperature—if
using a fan-assisted oven, follow the manufacturer's instructions
for adjusting the time and the temperature.

Vegetarians should ensure that cheeses are made with vegetarian
rennet. There are vegetarian forms of Parmesan, feta, Cheddar,
Cheshire, Monterey Jack, dolcelatte, goats' cheeses and many
others.

Contents

Introduction   6

Cook's tools   12

Soups and Starters   14

Fish   36

Chicken   62

Lamb and Pork   94

Utensils   104

Beef   118

Rice, grains, and pulses   130

Vegetarian   140

Vegetables, herbs, and fruit   158

Rice and Lentils   178

Spices   184

Breads and Accompaniments   196

Breads   212

Desserts   230

Index   252

Introduction

Indian cookery is not, in fact, the cuisine of a single nationality. It is, rather, the collective name given to the combination of different cuisines from many different countries.

India is a vast subcontinent, divided from the rest of Asia by the Himalayas. It is about the same size as all the countries of Europe put together, and has been home to an astonishing diversity of different peoples, speaking some 14 major languages and about 100 dialects. It is hardly surprising, then, that its cuisine should be correspondingly varied.

The influence of many different cultures, including those of the Moguls, Portuguese, Persians, and British, have, over the years, given rise to many new ideas in Indian cuisine. Each region has its own particular cooking traditions, which are based on the area's specific climate and soil. The various culinary features of each region combine to lend variety, excitement, and character to Indian cookery as a whole.

As a general rule, food tends to be hotter the further south you go. In more detail, the different regions can be characterized as follows.

Northern India

The Punjabi and Kashmiri styles of cooking come from the northern region of India. The north of the country is famous for its subtly spiced cooking, which owes much to the sophistication of the cooks at the luxurious courts of the Mughal emperors, who conquered northern India from Persia.

The Punjabis have the reputation of being gourmets and the best cooks in the country. The Punjab is particularly famous for its tandoori cooking and for many of its sweetmeats. Punjabis are keen wheat eaters, which they tend to consume in preference to rice.

Influenced by the Mughals, Kashmiri cooking is known for its meat cuisine. As a result, the curries that are produced in this area, which are made without any thickening agents such as onion and garlic, are close to perfection.

Ghee—clarified butter—is the most commonly used cooking fat throughout the northern part of India.

Southern India

The southern region of India is the stronghold of the Hindus. The Brahmins—who were the monitors of the Hindu faith and its temples—taught non-violence, or *ahimsa*, and thus advocated not eating meat. They declared the cow a sacred animal, which their followers were prohibited from eating.

The staple foods in the south of India are therefore vegetables and rice. Mustard oil is generally used as the cooking medium, and coconut, coconut milk, and tamarind are used in many of the local recipes. Curries from this part of India, which include the fierce vindaloo curries, are thin and fiery, using plenty of chiles.

sophisticated way of cooking. The Mughals ate meat, including the cow which was sacred for the Hindus, and their culinary influence is particularly evident in the regional meat dishes.

Eastern India

Eastern India—which encompasses Bengal and Bihar—is surrounded by rivers and seas. It is hardly surprising, therefore, that fish, which is both plentiful and inexpensive, should be such an important part of the local diet. Mustard oil is used as the principal cooking medium, which gives a slightly sweet flavor. Foods are spiced with mustard, cumin, anise, and fenugreek seeds. The easterners are known for their delicious sweetmeats and savories.

Western India

The cuisine of western India comes principally from Goa and Bombay. Goan food tends to be hot and spicy and uses a lot of coconut milk, vinegar, and tamarind juice. Dishes are cooked very slowly for a long time, which gives them a wonderfully rich flavor. Bombay is famed for its delicious fruit ice creams and for its refreshing cold drinks, made with fruit juices and yogurt, which are known as sharbats.

Central India

The cuisine from the central area of India is dominated by the Mughal influence, and is an especially refined and

Curries

Ask anyone in the West what first springs to mind when they think of Indian food and they are almost certain to say curry. The word curry is thought to come from the Tamil, or southern Indian, word *kari*, which means sauce, or from *karhai*, which is a commonly used Indian cooking vessel. Most curry sauces are characteristically aromatic, and are redolent of the rich blend of spices that are combined in them.

In India, the various ingredients that are used to make a curry depend largely on the taste of the individual who is preparing the dish. It is usual for all the ingredients, including spices, roots, and seeds, to be ground separately into a paste with a little water on what is known as a "curry stone." Once it has been made, a good curry powder will keep for years.

While there are many different flavors which recur frequently in curry making, such as coconut, ginger, onions, and tamarind, no dish can be called a curry if it does not contain a selection of spices. Many different spices are used in curries, all of them with a distinctive flavor, which is why there are so many different curries in India, for there is almost no limit to the possible combinations of spices.

Weights and measures are seldom used by Indian chefs. Much depends on the particular skill and judgment of the cook to produce the perfect aromatic curry, which must be neither too hot, nor too bland. The secret lies in finding the right proportions, which is something that can only come from experience. The traditional Indian culinary artiste guesses the quantities and gets perfect results every time.

Curry making owes a great deal to trial and error and you, too, can experiment with the quantities of spices you use. Indian chefs would never be limited by recipes, and these are only a guide. Use smaller quantities of these ingredients to start with, particularly if you are not yet used to Indian flavors, but always use them in the correct proportions, as instructed in the recipe.

Curry is the name given to a large group of dishes, produced in a number of different ways and with a wide range of different flavors. Some of these are wet; some dry; some are hot; some mild; some creamy; and some fruity. The range of different dishes is legendary.

Spices

Indians are skilled in using and blending spices—a skill that they have fortunately never lost over the years, in spite of their being influenced by so many other countries. Spices are dried aromatic parts of plants, including the seeds, leaves, roots, and bark. Their principal use is to flavor food.

The majority of spices are grown in tropical countries, though they are believed also to have been used in the eastern Mediterranean for some 5,000 years. The appeal of exotic spices used to be so great that they were once believed to be a gift worthy of royalty, and long hazardous journeys were undertaken in order to bring them back to Europe from faraway places such as China, Indonesia, and, of course, India.

It is a commonly held belief in India that spicy and exotic food makes the people who eat it more virile. Lord Krishna of India, for example, is said to have had some 16,000 wives, the implication being that he acquired his virility from the food he ate.

But it is wrong to think that Indian food should always be hot. Very hot food burns the palate, the skin on the tongue, and has a tendency to upset the stomach, particularly when eaten by someone who is unaccustomed to spicy food. Not all the spices that are used in India are hot. It is only the chiles and pepper that give a kick.

Dry-frying, or roasting spices brings out their distinctive flavors. It is usual in Indian cooking to dry-fry several whole spices at once, depending on what you will need in the recipe. Use a heavy-bottom skillet, put all the spices in an even layer into the skillet, and set over a moderate heat. Stir-fry the spices for about 5 minutes, until they are a shade or two darker and beginning to give off a delicious aroma. Allow the spices to cool, then grind them with a pestle and mortar. An electric coffee grinder, kept specially for the purpose, makes grinding whole spices much easier.

Vegetarian food

India has, for a long time, been regarded as the center of the vegetarian world. One reason for this may be because Hindus are forbidden by their religion to eat meat. In general, Indians are a peaceful people and have a great abhorrence for killing anything, including animals. Another cause could be economic reasons, vegetables being much less expensive than meat.

Ingredients

It is important always to use the very best ingredients possible. Where poultry, meat, and vegetables are concerned, the western cook is at an immediate advantage, since the quality is usually better than that available to his or her eastern counterpart.

But when it comes to the selection of Indian ingredients, it is important to take the utmost care. Unless you use the same ingredients as those that are used in India, you cannot expect to produce the same results.

This applies, in particular, to spices, which add a distinctive flavor and color.

Specialist Indian ingredients are now easily available from many food markets and Indian food stores. Because so many Indian people now live abroad and because of the proliferation of Indian restaurants, Indian food is enjoying a revival in popularity and many major cities now have speciality Indian stores. A look round these stores yields a fascinating glimpse into the rich diversity of Indian culture.

Another excellent source of Indian ingredients is your nearest large food market. People have become very interested in Indian food, with the result that a range of basic ingredients is often available. You will find special features throughout this book which supply detailed information about specialist Indian ingredients.

Basic ingredients

There are many ingredients that you will find in your kitchen closets and which will come in useful for Indian cookery. Some of these are included below.

Rice

Rice is highly nutritious and is an important accompaniment to curries. The particular type of rice most commonly used for Indian food is Patna or, as the native cook in India calls it, "table rice." It comes in various grades and qualities and is available either polished or unpolished. The best results will be obtained using the finest grade of unpolished Patna rice.

Basmati rice is another good Indian rice. It has small but long grains and a distinctive flavor. It is available in both brown and white versions.

Fat

The fat most commonly used in India is ghee, which is clarified butter—either buffalo or cow. Clarified means that all the milk solids have been removed. Ghee does not need to be refrigerated and is ideal for Indian cooking techniques, as it can be heated to a high temperature without burning.

Ghee was first developed in northern India, probably by nomadic peoples who had no regular crops of oil-rich foods and were in need of an easily transportable cooking fat. When it is properly made, it is absolutely free from moisture and impurities, and will neither splutter, nor burn or blacken. It has a particularly rich, nutty flavor.

In India, the best ghee is homemade. When it is sold in Indian markets it is often adulterated with nut oil and other fats. But pure ghee is expensive and, therefore, out of the reach of many ordinary people. Other fats, such as sesame oil, mustard oil, coconut oil, and cottonseed oil, are commonly used instead and virtually any neutral-flavored vegetable oil can be used. Corn and peanut oils are good all-purpose oils.

Ghee is available in the U.S. from some food markets and specialist food stores. It is sold in cans and keeps well for up to two or three months in the refrigerator.

Yogurt

Yogurt is often used to add a sharp creaminess to Indian curries. Use a plain yogurt, preferably a thin acidic-flavored variety rather then the milder, creamier Greek type. If you use a "set" yogurt, always stir it a little to break up the "setting" before adding it to the curry or serving it as an accompaniment.

Cooking utensils

Indian food can be cooked using all the usual utensils that you have in your kitchen, and you need very few—if any—special pieces of equipment. Cooking is often done using one utensil called a *karhai*, which is similar to the Chinese wok, its purpose being to use as little oil as possible. A saucepan or a heavy-based skillet will usually do just as well.

Fresh stock recipes

You will find it useful to have these basic recipes to hand as they are required throughout the book. A good stock is both easy and inexpensive to make, with only a few basic ingredients. A fresh aromatic broth is far superior to commercial bouillon cubes and, once it is made, a good stock can be frozen in small batches in plastic tubs or ice trays and used as required.

A few basic rules are necessary when making stock.
• Stock should always simmer extremely gently, or it will evaporate too quickly and become cloudy.
• Never add salt to the stock as simmering will reduce it

Coconut milk

Coconut milk is essential in Indian cookery. It can be made using either desiccated or fresh coconut, which gives a richer, more mellow flavor and a creamier consistency.

There is no need, nowadays and in this part of the world, to extract coconut milk from the coconut. Canned coconut milk is readily available in many food markets and gourmet food stores. It is unsweetened and works extremely well.

Coconut milk powder is also available, which needs to be mixed with water to produce coconut milk. Do this according to the packet instructions and add more or less water according to how thick or thin you want it to be.

Spices

A good selection of spices is essential. The most widely used of these include aniseed, asafetida, black onion seeds, cardamom, chiles, cinnamon, cloves, coriander seeds, cumin, fennel seeds, fenugreek, mustard seeds, nutmeg, saffron, and turmeric.

It is best to keep only small quantities of frequently used spices in the kitchen, and to store them in a cool, dry place. Use them within six months of buying, as a stale spice has very little to offer to any curry.

and concentrate the flavor. This will affect the overall flavor of the finished dish.

• Any scum that rises to the surface should be removed as it will spoil the color and flavor of the final stock.

• Avoid any floury root vegetables as these will cause the stock to become cloudy.

Chicken stock

The following recipe is light and delicately flavored.

• Chop a cooked chicken carcass into 3 or 4 pieces and place it in a large pot with the raw giblets and trimmings, 1 onion coarsely chopped, 2 large carrots coarsely chopped, 1 celery stalk coarsely chopped, 1 bay leaf, a few parsley stalks lightly crushed, and 1 sprig of thyme. Add 7 cups of cold water.

• Bring this to the boil, removing any scum from the surface. Lower the heat and simmer for 2–2½ hours. Strain the stock through a cheesecloth-lined strainer and leave to cool completely before refrigerating.

Makes 4½ cups
Preparation time: *5–10 minutes*
Cooking time: *about 1½ hours*

Fish stock

You should be able to get the bones for this stock from your local fish store, but avoid the bones of oily fish. It is important that this stock does not boil as it will become very cloudy.

• Place 3 pounds fish trimmings and 1 onion, sliced, the white part of 1 small leek, 1 celery stalk, sliced, 1 bay leaf, 6 parsley stalks, 10 whole peppercorns, and 2 cups of dry white wine in a large pot. Cover with 7 cups of cold water.

• Heat slowly until just below boiling point and simmer for 20 minutes, removing any scum from the surface. Strain the stock through a cheesecloth-lined strainer and leave to cool before refrigerating.

Makes 7 cups
Preparation time: *10 minutes*
Cooking time: *20 minutes*

Vegetable stock

This simple recipe makes a well-flavored vegetable stock. You can introduce changes according to which vegetables are in season.

• Place 1 pound chopped mixed vegetables, such as carrots, leeks, celery, onion, or mushrooms, in a large saucepan. Add 1 garlic clove, 6 peppercorns, and 1 bouquet garni (2 parsley sprigs, 2 thyme sprigs, and 1 bay leaf). Cover with 5 cups water.

• Bring to the boil, then reduce the heat and simmer gently for 30 minutes, skimming the surface of the stock, when necessary. Strain the stock and allow to cool completely before refrigerating.

Makes 4½ cups
Preparation time: *5–10 minutes*
Cooking time: *about 45 minutes*

Cook's tools

There are so many good things and good people in India,
that what they eat is no mean study,
for food often maketh man.

Lt.Gen. Sir George MacMunn,
K.C.B., K.C.S.I., D.S.O.

In Indian cooking, kitchen tools are relatively basic, and you will probably already have most of the equipment you need in your kitchen.

Colander
The colander is used for separating liquids from solids, and for draining and rinsing food. Although colanders come in many different shapes and sizes, they are basically a container with holes and are usually made of plastic or stainless steel. A colander is ideal for rinsing food and for draining rice and vegetables.

Grater
Graters come in either a box shape or a single flat sheet. Both shapes have perforations which perform different functions. The fine holes are for grating spices and rind, the medium and large holes are for grating cheese and vegetables. Graters are generally made of stainless steel, as it is hard-wearing and does not rust. If you have a flat sheet grater, insure that the grater is properly balanced when grating, as this sort does have a tendency to slip.

Mixing bowl
A mixing bowl should be wide enough to allow mixtures to be beaten or gently folded. The bowl should be rested on a grip stand to prevent it slipping.

Rolling pin
A rolling pin is used for rolling out bread dough or pastry to a smooth, flat, even sheet. It should be heavy so that it—rather than you—does the work. A rolling pin can be made of wood, plastic, nylon, or marble, and should be wide and well balanced. When rolling out any mixture, use flour to stop the mixture sticking to the pin. Wipe the rolling pin clean before storing it.

Chopping board
As its name suggests, the chopping board is a surface that is used for chopping food, including meat, vegetables, and fruit. It should be made from a material that is soft enough not to blunt a knife, but hard enough to resist splintering. Boards are generally made of wood, or a synthetic material. Wooden boards require sanding and oiling in order to maintain them. Some cooks prefer a synthetic material, such as plastic, as it is easier to keep clean and sterile. Whichever material you choose, your board should be as large as you have room for on your work surface.

Pestle and mortar
A pestle and mortar are essentially a grinder with a bowl, and are among the earliest grinding tools known to man. Such a utensil has been in use for thousands of years for grinding herbs and spices, and is still widely used today as it is so efficient. Pestles and mortars come in many different sizes, according to needs, and can be made of ceramic, stone, wood, or metal. The insides of the bowl should be rough and unglazed.

Knives (chopping, paring)
A good cook is not equipped without a set of good kitchen knives. Knives should always be well maintained, cleaned, thoroughly dried, and sharpened regularly.

Chopping knife: A heavy, wide-blade knife, this is ideal for chopping all vegetables and other ingredients. It is also good for flattening thinly sliced meats, and transferring ingredients from the board to the pan.

Paring knife: This is a small, sharp knife, which is used for trimming and peeling fruit and vegetables.

Soups and
Starters

Fish and Coconut Soup

1 pound anglerfish or halibut fillet, skinned and cubed

⅓ cup desiccated coconut

6 shallots or 1 small onion

6 almonds, blanched

2 garlic cloves, peeled

1-inch piece of fresh ginger root, peeled and sliced

2 lemon grass stalks, trimmed

2–3 teaspoons turmeric

3 tablespoons oil

1 fresh red chile, seeded and sliced

salt

fresh cilantro leaves, to garnish

Coconut milk

3½ cups desiccated coconut

3 cups boiling water

Coconut cream

3½ cups desiccated coconut

3 cups boiling water

make the coconut milk by placing the desiccated coconut and boiling water in a blender or food processor. Blend for 20 seconds. Pour into a bowl and leave to cool to blood temperature. Strain into a clean bowl or pitcher.

repeat the above process to make the coconut cream, letting the strained liquid stand. When the cream rises to the top of the milk, skim it off—this is the coconut cream.

sprinkle the fish with salt. Place the coconut in a wok and heat gently until it is golden and crisp. Remove from the wok and pound until oily. Set aside.

purée the shallots (or onion), almonds, garlic, ginger, and 2½ inches from the root end of the lemon grass stalks (reserving the remainder) in a blender or food processor. Add the turmeric.

heat the oil in a wok or saucepan and cook the puréed mixture for a few minutes. Add the coconut milk and bring to the boil, stirring constantly. Stir in the fish, chile, and the remaining lemon grass. Cook over a gentle heat for about 5 minutes.

stir in the pounded coconut and cook for a further 5 minutes. Remove the lemon grass stalks and stir in the coconut cream. Serve hot, garnished with cilantro.

Serves 4
Preparation time: *25 minutes*
Cooking time: *15–20 minutes*

Spiced Chicken Soup

6¼ cups water
1 x 2½-pound chicken, quartered
4 unpeeled raw jumbo shrimp
2 macadamia nuts, chopped
4 shallots or 1 small onion, chopped
2 garlic cloves, minced
2 teaspoons grated fresh ginger root
pinch of turmeric
pinch of chili powder
vegetable oil for shallow frying
1 tablespoon light soy sauce
3 ounces bean sprouts
1 potato, thinly sliced
salt and freshly ground black pepper

put the water in a large saucepan and bring to the boil. Add the chicken and shrimp with a little seasoning, then cover and simmer gently for 40 minutes. Strain, reserving 5 cups of the liquid. Shred the meat from the chicken and peel and chop the shrimp.

blend the macadamias, shallots (or onion), garlic, and ginger to a purée in a blender or food processor. Add the turmeric and chili powder and mix well. Alternatively, pound in a mortar.

heat 2 tablespoons of oil in a saucepan, add the spice paste and fry for a few seconds. Stir in 1¼ cups of the reserved liquid, the soy sauce, chicken, and shrimp. Simmer for 10 minutes. Add the remaining liquid and simmer for a further 10 minutes. Add the bean sprouts and cook for 3 minutes.

fry the potato slices in some hot oil, while the soup is cooking, until golden and crisp. Remove and drain on paper towels. Season the hot soup and serve garnished with the fried potato.

Serves 4–6
Preparation time: *20 minutes*
Cooking time: *1¼ hours*

clipboard: The macadamia nut is the fruit of an Australian tree, which has a flavor reminiscent of coconut. It is often used in curries in Indian cookery.

Indian Split Pea Soup

This chilled soup is easy to make and is a deliciously refreshing soup for a hot summer's day. It looks pretty garnished with cucumber, scallions, and mint.

1⅓ cups yellow split peas
5½ cups water
½ teaspoon turmeric
2 tablespoons lemon juice
1 fresh green chile, seeded and finely chopped
1 teaspoon ground cumin
1 teaspoon ground coriander seeds
½ small cucumber
3 scallions
6 tablespoons plain yogurt
salt and freshly ground black pepper
fresh mint leaves, to garnish

pick over the yellow split peas to remove any grit and then wash under running cold water and drain them in a colander.

place the drained split peas in a large saucepan with the water and turmeric and bring to the boil. Reduce the heat and cover the pan. Simmer very gently for 1¼–1½ hours until cooked and tender. Remove from the heat.

tip the split peas and their liquid into a large blender or food processor. Add the lemon juice, seasoning, chile, cumin, and coriander seeds and blend until smooth. If the soup is a little too thick, thin it down with water or more lemon juice. Transfer to a serving bowl and refrigerate until required.

dice the cucumber and slice the scallions just before serving. Swirl the yogurt into the chilled soup and serve garnished with the cucumber, scallions, and mint.

Serves 4
Preparation time: *20 minutes*
Cooking time: *1¼–1½ hours*

Spiced Pea Soup

This creamy soup has a mild spicy flavor, thanks to the addition of ginger, cumin, coriander, and chile. It is a delicate green color, garnished with fresh cilantro leaves.

2 tablespoons ghee or 1 tablespoon vegetable oil
1 large onion, coarsely chopped
2 garlic cloves, minced
1 small potato, diced
1-inch piece of fresh ginger root, peeled and sliced
1 teaspoon ground cumin seeds
1 teaspoon ground coriander seeds
3¾ cups Vegetable Stock (see page 11)
2 cups fresh or frozen peas
1 fresh green chile, chopped
1¼ cups light cream
salt and freshly ground black pepper
fresh cilantro leaves, to garnish

heat the ghee or oil in a large heavy-bottom saucepan and sauté the onion and garlic gently for about 5 minutes, until soft and golden.

add the potato, ginger, ground cumin, and coriander and stir well. Continue cooking gently over a low heat for a few minutes, stirring until the potato is well coated with spices.

pour in the vegetable stock and bring to the boil. Reduce the heat, cover the pan, and simmer gently for 15 minutes. Add the peas and chile, and season to taste with salt and pepper. Continue cooking for 5 minutes over a low heat.

blend the soup in a food processor or blender until smooth and return to the pan. Place over a low heat and stir in the cream. Serve hot, garnished with cilantro leaves.

Serves 4
Preparation time: *15 minutes*
Cooking time: *35–40 minutes*

clipboard: Ghee is used as a cooking fat in Indian cookery. It is clarified butter, the best being made from buffaloes' milk, which is twice as rich in fat as cows' milk. Clarified butter, which has had all the milk solids removed, can be heated to a high temperature without burning.

Ground Meat Samosas

2 tablespoons milk
oil for deep frying
chutney, to serve

Dough
4½ cups all-purpose flour
1 teaspoon salt
¾ cup soft margarine
⅝ cup water

Filling
1 tablespoon butter
1 small onion, chopped
½ teaspoon cumin seeds
1 cup ground beef
1 fresh green chile, finely chopped
1 teaspoon salt
1 cup cooked peas
1 teaspoon chopped fresh cilantro leaves
freshly ground black pepper

Serves 6
Preparation time: *1 hour*
Cooking time: *15–20 minutes*

sift the flour and salt into a large mixing bowl to make the samosa dough. Cut the margarine into small pieces and rub it into the flour with your fingertips, until the mixture resembles fine bread crumbs. Stir in the water, a little at a time, until it is all amalgamated. Knead thoroughly until you have a smooth dough. Cover with a damp cloth

make the filling by melting the butter in a saucepan. Sauté the onion and cumin seeds over a moderate heat, stirring occasionally for 5–7 minutes. Add the ground beef, chile, and salt and mix thoroughly. Reduce the heat and simmer for 10 minutes.

stir in the peas and continue cooking over a moderate heat for 5 minutes, or until the liquid has evaporated. Remove the pan from the heat and mix in the cilantro and a pinch of pepper. Let cool before using to stuff the samosas.

divide the samosa dough into 12 equal portions and roll out each one to a thin circle, 7 inches in diameter. Cut each circle in half with a sharp knife and then cover the semicircles with a damp cloth while you fill them one at a time.

brush the edges of each semicircle with a little milk and spoon some filling on to the center. Fold in the corners, overlapping them to form a cone. Fold over and seal the top to make a triangle. Deep fry in hot oil in batches, until crisp and golden. Drain on paper towels and serve hot with chutney.

Vegetable Samosas

These crisp and spicy vegetable pastries are absolutely delicious served as an appetizer, accompanied by your favorite chutney.

1 quantity basic samosa dough (see Ground Meat Samosas, page 24)
2 tablespoons milk
oil for deep frying
chutney, to serve

Filling
1 tablespoon ghee, or vegetable oil
pinch of asafetida powder
2 teaspoons mustard seeds
1 pound potatoes, parboiled and diced
1 cup cooked peas
2 fresh green chiles, seeded and chopped
1 teaspoon salt
1 teaspoon pomegranate seeds (optional)
1 teaspoon garam masala
2 tablespoons chopped fresh cilantro leaves

make the filling: heat the ghee or oil in a skillet and add the asafetida powder, mustard seeds, potatoes, peas, chiles, salt, and pomegranate seeds, if using. Stir well over a moderate heat for 2 minutes. Cover the pan, reduce the heat, and cook gently for 10 minutes.

remove the pan from the heat and add the garam masala and chopped cilantro. Stir well and then leave the filling to cool before using to stuff the samosas.

roll out the samosa dough and prepare the semicircles as described previously (see Ground Meat Samosas, page 24). Use the vegetable filling to stuff the samosas and fold over, sealing the edges with milk. Remember to cover them with a damp cloth while you are assembling them.

heat the oil for deep frying and then fry the samosas, a few at a time, until crisp and golden. Remove with a slotted spoon and drain on paper towels. Serve them hot with chutney.

Serves 6
Preparation time: *1 hour*
  (including making dough)
Cooking time: *10 minutes*

Spiced Fried Shrimp

Marinated in tamarind water with a little turmeric, ginger, garlic, and light soy sauce, these are an Eastern variation on shrimp fritters.

1 pound cooked shrimp
2 tablespoons tamarind water, or lemon juice
pinch of turmeric
1 teaspoon grated fresh ginger root
2 shallots or ½ onion, sliced
2 garlic cloves, minced
1 tablespoon light soy sauce
⅝ cup oil for frying

Batter
¾ cup rice flour or all-purpose flour
4 tablespoons water
1 small egg, beaten
salt and freshly ground black pepper

remove the shells from the shrimp, leaving the tails intact. Carefully remove the black vein that runs along the back of each shrimp.

place the shrimp in a bowl with the tamarind water, turmeric, ginger, shallots or onion, garlic, and soy sauce. Stir well and set aside to marinate in a cool place for 30 minutes.

make the batter while the shrimp are marinating. Put the flour in a bowl and gradually add the water. Season with a little salt and pepper and then beat in the egg. Beat lightly until the batter is smooth and free from lumps.

drain the marinade from the shrimp and shallots and then dip them into the batter. Heat the oil in a skillet or wok and fry the shrimp and shallots in batches until crisp and golden on both sides. Remove and drain on paper towels. Serve hot with plain boiled rice or some hot sauce or chutney.

Serves 4
Preparation time: *15 minutes*, plus
   30 minutes marinating time
Cooking time: *10 minutes*

Ekuri

You thought you knew everything there was to know about scrambled eggs, but that was before you tried this delicious Indian version, lightly spiced with fresh green chiles.

4 tablespoons butter
1 onion, finely chopped
2 fresh green chiles, finely chopped
8 eggs, lightly beaten with 2 tablespoons water
1 tablespoon finely chopped fresh cilantro leaves
salt

heat the butter in a pan, add the onion and fry until deep golden. Add the chiles and fry for 30 seconds, then add the eggs, cilantro, and salt to taste. Cook, stirring until the eggs are scrambled and set. Serve hot.

Serves 4
Preparation time: *5 minutes*
Cooking time: *10 minutes*

clipboard: Chiles first grew in the Amazon region of South America and in Mexico, and it was some time before they reached India. The arrival of the chile changed the flavor of Indian cooking. Until then, the only source of "heat" had been the peppercorn and the mustard seed. Fresh chiles are easily available, either green, yellow, or red, from food markets. The inner membrane and the seeds are the hottest part, so it is advisable to wear gloves when you remove them. Slit the chile lengthwise down the center, hold it under a cold tap, and rub off the membrane and seeds. Whenever you handle chiles, be careful not to put your fingers anywhere near your eyes, as the pungent juices will irritate and sting them.

Pakora

Pakora are onion rings, spinach leaves, and parboiled potatoes, which are dipped into a spicy batter and deep-fried until crisp and golden. Absolutely delicious!

1 cup garbanzo bean or gram (besan) flour
1 teaspoon salt
½ teaspoon chili powder
about ⅝ cup water
2 fresh green chiles, finely chopped
1 tablespoon finely chopped fresh cilantro leaves
1 teaspoon melted ghee or vegetable oil
oil for deep frying
2 onions, sliced into rings
8 small fresh spinach leaves, washed
2–3 potatoes, parboiled and sliced

sift the flour, salt, and chili powder into a bowl. Stir in sufficient water to make a thick batter and beat well until smooth. Let stand for 30 minutes.

stir the chiles and cilantro into the batter, then add the melted ghee or vegetable oil. Drop in the onion rings to coat thickly with batter.

heat the oil in a deep pan, drop in the onion rings, and deep fry until crisp and golden. Remove from the pan with a slotted spoon, drain on paper towels, and keep warm.

dip the spinach leaves into the batter and deep fry in the same way, adding more oil to the pan if necessary. Finally, repeat the process with the potato slices. Serve hot.

Serves 4
Preparation time: *10 minutes*, plus
  standing time
Cooking time: *35 minutes*

clipboard: Cilantro has bright green, lacy leaves and white flowers, and an intense flavor and perfume. The leaves, roots, and seeds are all used in cooking, and the leaves make a particularly attractive garnish. Gram flour (also known as besun or chana dhaal flour) is made from lentils and is useful for people who are allergic to gluten, a component of all wheat products.

Shrimp Kebobs

Jumbo Pacific shrimp are not cheap but they're succulent and tasty. To prepare this dish, they're marinated in lemon juice and spices, and then quickly broiled on skewers.

2 tablespoons oil
1 tablespoon lemon juice
2 garlic cloves, minced
1 teaspoon paprika
½ teaspoon chili powder
½ teaspoon salt
½ teaspoon turmeric
1 tablespoon finely chopped fresh cilantro leaves
12 jumbo Pacific shrimp, peeled

place all the ingredients in a shallow dish, stirring to coat the shrimp thoroughly. Cover and chill for several hours, stirring occasionally.

thread the shrimp on to skewers or place in the broiler pan, and cook under a preheated moderate broiler for 3–4 minutes on each side, or until cooked. Spoon over the pan juices when turning.

Serves 4
Preparation time: 5 *minutes*, plus
2–3 hours chilling time
Cooking time: 6–8 *minutes*

clipboard: Turmeric grows wild in the tropical countries of southern Asia and belongs to the same family as ginger. It is often used in marinades and gives an attractive yellow coloring, reminiscent of saffron. Because of its color, turmeric is also used as a dye, most notably in the yellow robes of Buddhist monks.

Fish

Fish in Coconut Milk

2 cloves, ground

4 green cardamoms, ground

2 fresh green chiles, crushed

2 garlic cloves, minced

½-inch piece of fresh ginger root, peeled and chopped

1 tablespoon vindaloo masala powder

lemon juice to mix

1 pound white fish fillets (e.g. sole, flounder)

2 tablespoons vegetable oil

1 onion, thinly sliced

1¼ cups unsweetened coconut milk

salt

1 tablespoon chopped fresh cilantro leaves, to garnish

mix together the cloves, cardamoms, chiles, garlic, ginger, vindaloo masala powder, and a little salt in a bowl. Stir in enough lemon juice to make a smooth, thick paste.

rinse the fish fillets and pat them dry with paper towels. Spread the prepared spicy paste thickly and evenly over the fish.

heat the oil in a large saucepan or deep skillet, and fry the onion until soft and golden. Add the prepared fish fillets and fry on both sides until golden brown.

pour in the coconut milk and season to taste with salt. Cover the pan and cook gently over a low heat for 15 minutes. Serve the fish sprinkled with cilantro.

Serves 4
Preparation time: *20 minutes*
Cooking time: *30 minutes*

clipboard: Coconut milk is essential in Indian cookery (see page 16). It can be made using either desiccated or fresh coconut, which gives a richer, more mellow flavor and a creamier consistency. But there is no need nowadays to extract coconut milk from the coconut. Canned coconut milk is widely available in food markets and gourmet food stores. It is unsweetened and works extremely well.

Curried Fish Balls

1½ pounds white fish fillets (e.g. haddock, scrod, cod)
2 tablespoons lemon juice
1 egg
1½ teaspoons salt
½ cup garbanzo bean or gram (besan) flour
4 fresh green chiles, seeded and chopped
1 onion, finely chopped
2 tablespoons bread crumbs
vegetable oil for shallow frying
freshly ground black pepper

Sauce
½ cup ghee or 2½ tablespoons vegetable oil
1 large onion, thinly sliced
2 garlic cloves, thinly sliced
1 cinnamon stick
2 bay leaves
2 teaspoons ground cumin
2 teaspoons ground coriander
1½ teaspoons turmeric
1 teaspoon chili powder
5 ounces tomato paste
2½ cups Fish Stock (see page 11)
2 tablespoons lemon juice
½ cup desiccated coconut
seeds of 10 cardamoms, ground
2 teaspoons fenugreek seeds, ground
salt and freshly ground black pepper

arrange the fish fillets in an ovenproof dish and sprinkle with lemon juice. Cover with foil and stand in a roasting pan half-filled with water. Poach in a preheated oven at 325°F for 15 minutes. Remove and, when cool, flake the fish.

whisk the egg with the salt and a little pepper. Sift in the gram flour, whisking all the time until the batter is smooth.

add the flaked fish, chiles, onion, and bread crumbs to the batter. Stir well to make a stiff paste. Break off lumps and form into about 20 small balls. Heat the oil in a skillet and shallow fry the balls in batches until evenly browned. Drain and keep warm.

make the sauce: heat the ghee or oil and fry the onion and garlic for 5 minutes, until soft. Add all the spices and cook for 2 minutes. Add the tomato paste and bring to the boil. Add the remaining ingredients and cook over a medium heat for 10 minutes. Add the fish balls, simmer for 5 minutes, and serve hot with rice.

Serves 4
Preparation time: *30 minutes*
Cooking time: *40 minutes*
Oven temperature: 325°F

clipboard: Garbanzo beans are a rich source of carbohydrates, proteins, phosphorus, calcium, and iron, and therefore deserve a place in any healthy diet. In India, they are ground into flour, which is also known as gram flour or besan. Garbanzo flour is available in larger food markets and gourmet food stores.

Charcoal-Broiled Fish

2–3½ pounds halibut, cleaned and washed
4 tablespoons lemon juice
2 teaspoons salt
1½ teaspoons freshly ground black pepper

Masala
1 large onion, peeled
1 garlic clove, peeled
1 tablespoon chopped fresh cilantro leaves
4 teaspoons plain yogurt
2 teaspoons garam masala
1 teaspoon chili powder
1 teaspoon ground coriander
1 teaspoon ground cumin
1 teaspoon ground fenugreek

line a large baking dish with a sheet of foil 2½ times the size of the fish. Make 4 or 5 deep cuts in each side of the fish. Rub the fish with lemon juice and sprinkle with salt and pepper. Place the fish on the foil and set this aside.

make the masala: put the onion and garlic in a food processor and chop them finely. Alternatively, chop them very finely with a knife or shred them on a shredder.

place the onion and garlic in a bowl with the coriander, yogurt, garam masala, chili powder, ground coriander, cumin, and the fenugreek, and mix well.

smear this mixture over the fish and inside the cuts and the cavity. Draw up the sides of the foil to make a tent shape and seal the edges. Leave in a cool place to marinate for 4 hours.

bake in a preheated oven at 325°F for 20 minutes. Remove the fish carefully and finish cooking on a barbecue or on a wire rack in the oven.

Serves 4
Preparation time: *15 minutes*, plus
  4 hours marinating time
Cooking time: *25–30 minutes*
Oven temperature: 325°F

Fish Tandoori

A delicately flavored yogurt tandoori marinade goes particularly well with fish. It is possible to buy ready-prepared tandoori marinades, but this homemade version is a winner.

4 halibut or white fish steaks, about 6 ounces each
¼ cup plain yogurt
2 tablespoons oil
2 tablespoons paprika
1 tablespoon ground cumin
1 teaspoon ground fennel seeds
1 teaspoon chili powder
salt

To garnish
1 small lettuce, shredded
1 fennel bulb, sliced
lemon wedges

wash the halibut steaks under running cold water and then gently pat them dry with paper towels. Set aside while you prepare the tandoori mixture.

put the yogurt in a bowl with the oil, paprika, cumin, fennel seeds, chili powder, and a little salt. Mix well together.

place the halibut steaks in the bowl and rub well with the tandoori mixture. Cover the bowl and leave in a cool place to marinate for 4–5 hours.

transfer the marinated fish to a shallow, ovenproof baking dish. Bake uncovered in a preheated oven at 350°F for 20–25 minutes. Arrange the lettuce on a warm serving dish and place the fish on top. Spoon over the juices and serve garnished with lettuce, fennel, and lemon wedges.

Serves 4
Preparation time: *15 minutes*, plus
  4–5 hours marinating time
Cooking time: *20–25 minutes*
Oven temperature: 350°F

Fish Kebobs

Fish kebobs need to be made with a fairly firm white fish, such as haddock, halibut, or anglerfish, or they will disintegrate too easily and will fall off the skewers.

2-inch piece of fresh ginger root, crushed

1 garlic clove, minced

2 teaspoons ground cumin

1 teaspoon freshly ground black pepper

1 teaspoon ground coriander

1 teaspoon garam masala

½ teaspoon ground cloves

1 teaspoon ground aniseed

6 tablespoons plain yogurt

2 pounds white fish fillets, skinned and cubed

4 small onions, peeled

oil for basting

To serve

lime wedges

Raita (see page 208)

fresh mint leaves

put the ginger, garlic, cumin, black pepper, coriander, garam masala, cloves, and aniseed in a large bowl. Stir in the yogurt and mix together until well blended.

add the pieces of fish to the yogurt mixture and turn in the marinade. Leave in a cool place for at least 1 hour.

cut the onions into thick slices. Thread them on to some wooden kebob skewers, alternating with the marinated fish.

brush the kebobs with any remaining yogurt marinade and a little oil. Arrange on a broiler pan and place under a preheated hot broiler until cooked and lightly browned all over. Turn the kebobs occasionally and baste with oil and marinade as necessary. Serve with lime wedges and yogurt raita, scattered with fresh mint.

Serves 4
Preparation time: *15 minutes*, plus
1 hour marinating time
Cooking time: *10-15 minutes*

clipboard: Aniseed, also known as anise, has a strong licorice-like flavor, which is loved by some but hated by others. It is often used in India in marinades and curries, particularly with fish.

Shrimp Curry
with onion and garlic

4 tablespoons ghee or 1 tablespoon vegetable oil

1 small onion, sliced

2 garlic cloves, sliced

2 teaspoons ground coriander

½ teaspoon ground ginger

1 teaspoon turmeric

½ teaspoon ground cumin

½ teaspoon chili powder

2 tablespoons vinegar

1 pound peeled shrimp

¾ cup water

chopped fresh cilantro leaves, to garnish

heat the ghee or oil in a large heavy-bottom saucepan. Add the onion and garlic and sauté gently over a low heat for 4–5 minutes, until golden and soft.

mix together the ground coriander, ginger, turmeric, cumin, and chili powder in a small bowl. Mix in the vinegar to make a smooth paste.

add the spicy paste to the onion and garlic mixture in the pan, and then sauté gently for a further 3 minutes, stirring constantly with a wooden spoon.

tip in the shrimp and turn gently with a wooden spoon until they are well coated with the spices. Stir in the water and then simmer over a gentle heat for 2–3 minutes. Serve immediately, garnished with cilantro leaves, with plain boiled rice.

Serves 4
Preparation time: *15 minutes*
Cooking time: *12–15 minutes*

clipboard: Cumin is one of the most subtle and delicate of all the Indian spices. It blends remarkably well with coriander and other spices, such as ginger and turmeric, as in this recipe. It perfectly complements shrimp and fish.

Barbecued Jumbo Shrimp

1 pound jumbo shrimp
8 tablespoons lemon juice
1½ teaspoons salt
1½ teaspoons freshly ground black pepper
1 teaspoon aniseed

Marinade
2 teaspoons coriander seeds
2 teaspoons fenugreek seeds
seeds of 20 cardamoms
1½ teaspoons black onion seeds (kalongi)
4 bay leaves
1 large onion, chopped
3 garlic cloves, chopped
3-inch piece of fresh ginger root, peeled and chopped
1½ cups plain yogurt
1½ teaspoons turmeric
¼ cup melted ghee or vegetable oil
few drops of red food coloring

wash the shrimp and remove the heads. Make a slit along the underside of each shell with a sharp knife and then slightly flatten each shrimp. Place in a bowl and sprinkle with the lemon juice, salt, and pepper. Mix well and then set aside.

make the marinade: spread the coriander, fenugreek, cardamom, and black onion seeds on a cookie sheet. Add the bay leaves and place in a preheated oven at 400°F for 10–15 minutes. Remove and cool, then grind with a mortar and pestle.

place the onion, garlic, and ginger in a blender or food processor with the yogurt and turmeric, and blend until smooth. Add the ground roasted spices and melted ghee or vegetable oil and blend again for 30 seconds. Add the food coloring.

pour the marinade over the shrimp, cover, and marinate in the refrigerator for 6–8 hours or overnight. Remove the shrimp and thread on to skewers. Sprinkle with aniseed and barbecue (or broil) gently for about 5 minutes, turning frequently and brushing with the marinade. Serve hot.

Serves 4
Preparation time: *30 minutes*, plus
 6–8 hours marinating time
Cooking time: *5–10 minutes*
Oven temperature: 400°F

Spicy Steamed Mussels
with coconut and yogurt

2 pounds fresh mussels

½ cup ghee or 2½ tablespoons vegetable oil

1 large onion, finely chopped

2 garlic cloves, finely chopped

2 teaspoons desiccated coconut

2 teaspoons salt

1 teaspoon turmeric

1 teaspoon chili powder

1 teaspoon freshly ground black pepper

⅝ cup vinegar

2 cups plain yogurt

2 teaspoons garam masala

8 tablespoons lemon juice

fresh cilantro leaves, to garnish

scrub the mussels under cold running water and remove the "beards." Place in a large bowl, cover with fresh cold water, and leave to soak for 20–30 minutes.

heat the ghee or oil in a large saucepan while the mussels are soaking; add the onion and garlic and sauté gently for 5 minutes, or until soft. Add the coconut and salt and continue cooking until the coconut begins to brown. Stir in the turmeric, chili powder, and pepper and cook for 1 further minute.

drain the mussels and discard any that are open. Add the vinegar and mussels to the pan, cover, and turn up the heat. Cook over a high heat for 5 minutes, shaking the pan occasionally, until the mussels open. Remove from the heat. Discard any mussels that have not opened.

remove the empty half shells from the mussels and discard. Arrange the mussels in layers in a warm serving dish. Pour the cooking liquid into a blender or food processor, add the yogurt and garam masala, and blend for 1 minute. Return to the pan and heat through without boiling. Pour over the mussels and serve, sprinkled with lemon juice and cilantro.

Serves 4
Preparation time: *20 minutes*, plus
 20–30 minutes soaking time
Cooking time: *10–12 minutes*

Baked Spiced Fish

Cod steaks are cooked in an interesting spice mixture, consisting of ginger, cloves, chiles, chili powder, cilantro leaves, and lemon juice, to make a delicious combination of flavors.

4 tablespoons oil

4 ounces shredded fresh coconut

2-inch piece of fresh ginger root, chopped

1 large onion, chopped

4 garlic cloves, finely chopped

2 fresh green chiles, seeded and chopped

1 teaspoon chili powder

2 tablespoons finely chopped fresh cilantro leaves

4 tablespoons lemon juice

2 pounds cod or white fish steaks

salt

heat the oil in a pan, add the coconut, ginger, onion, garlic, chiles, and chili powder and fry gently until the onion is translucent. Add the cilantro, lemon juice, and salt to taste and simmer for 15 minutes, or until the coconut is soft.

oil the bottom of a baking dish just large enough to hold the fish. Arrange the fish steaks side by side and pour over the spice mixture.

bake in a preheated moderate oven at 325°F for 25 minutes, or until the cod steaks are cooked and tender.

Serves 4
Preparation time: *35 minutes*
Cooking time: *40 minutes*
Oven temperature: 325°F

clipboard: Along with the West Indies and west Africa, India is one of the largest growers of ginger for export. It is essential in many Indian dishes and is also used in baths for toning the system and for relieving muscular aches and pains.

Amotik

Tamarind is used in this mildly spiced fish dish to add a distinctive bittersweet flavor. Be particularly careful not to overcook the fish or it will disintegrate.

2 ounces tamarind, soaked in 6 tablespoons
hot water for 30 minutes
4 tablespoons oil
1½ pounds anglerfish or other firm white fish, cubed
flour, for dusting
I onion, chopped
4 fresh green chiles, finely chopped
2 garlic cloves, minced
I teaspoon ground cumin seeds
½–I teaspoon chili powder
I tablespoon vinegar
salt

strain the tamarind, squeezing out as much water as possible. Discard the tamarind and reserve the water.

heat the oil in a large pan. Lightly dust the fish with flour, add to the pan, and sauté quickly on both sides. Remove from the pan with a slotted spoon and set aside.

add the onion to the pan and cook until soft and golden. Add the tamarind water, chiles, garlic, cumin, chili powder, and salt to taste and cook for 10 minutes. Add the fish and any juices and the vinegar.

simmer, uncovered, for about 5 minutes.

Serves 4
Preparation time: *20 minutes*
Cooking time: about *20 minutes*

clipboard: The tamarind is a tall, evergreen tree which has been cultivated in India for centuries. Yellow flowers are followed by light brown, hairy pods, containing some 4–10 seeds surrounded by a sticky dark red paste. Tamarind can be bought either fresh, in rectangular blocks of compressed pulp and seeds, or as a thick concentrate which is less easily available in the shops. The compressed form, which is used in this recipe, has to be soaked for between 30 minutes and 1 hour.

Shrimp Pilau

Basmati rice is a special variety of Indian rice, with small but long grains and a distinctive flavor. It is much prized by the Indians and is the best rice to use for this pilau.

1½ cups Basmati rice

6 tablespoons ghee or vegetable oil

1 tablespoon coriander seeds, crushed

½ teaspoon turmeric

1 small pineapple, cubed or 1 x 8-oz can pineapple cubes, drained

8 ounces frozen shrimp, thawed

1 teaspoon salt

about 2½ cups Fish or Chicken Stock (see page 11)

To garnish

2 tablespoons ghee or vegetable oil

2 tablespoons golden raisins

2 tablespoons cashews

2 hard-boiled eggs, quartered

2 tablespoons chopped fresh cilantro leaves

wash the rice under cold running water, then soak in cold water for 30 minutes; drain thoroughly.

heat the ghee or vegetable oil in a large saucepan, add the coriander seeds and fry for 30 seconds. Add the turmeric and stir for a few seconds, then add the pineapple and cook, stirring for 30 seconds. Add the shrimp, rice, and salt. (If using a stock cube, omit the salt.) Fry, stirring, for 1 minute, then pour in enough stock to cover the rice by ¼ inch. Bring to the boil, cover tightly, and cook very gently for 25 minutes, or until the rice is cooked and the liquid absorbed.

prepare the garnish while the rice is cooking: heat the ghee or corn oil in a small pan, add the golden raisins and cashews and fry for 1–2 minutes until the golden raisins are plump and the cashews lightly colored.

transfer the rice to a warmed serving dish and gently fork in the golden raisins and cashews. Arrange the egg quarters around the edge and sprinkle the cilantro on top.

Serves 6
Preparation time: *10 minutes*, plus
30 minutes soaking time
Cooking time: *about 45 minutes*

Fish Fritters

These lightly spiced cod fritters are perfect for tempting the taste buds. Neither too hot nor too bland, they are certain to satisfy even the fussiest of eaters.

6 tablespoons oil
2 onions, chopped
1 tablespoon ground coriander seeds
3 fresh green chiles, seeded and chopped
1 teaspoon salt
1 teaspoon freshly ground black pepper
1½ pounds cod or white fish fillets, skinned and cut into small pieces
2 tablespoons finely chopped fresh cilantro leaves

Batter
1 cup garbanzo bean or gram flour (besan)
½ teaspoon chili powder
½ teaspoon salt
1 egg, beaten
7 tablespoons water

heat 3 tablespoons of the oil in a pan, add the onion, and fry until just soft. Stir in the ground coriander, chiles, salt, and pepper, then add the fish. Fry for 2 minutes, then cover and cook over a very low heat for 2 minutes. Break up the mixture with a fork and add the chopped cilantro. Remove from the heat and set aside while making the batter.

sift the flour, chili powder, and salt into a bowl. Add the egg and water and beat well to make a smooth batter. Let stand for 30 minutes, then stir in the fish mixture.

heat the remaining oil in a skillet and drop in small spoonfuls of the batter mixture. Fry on both sides until golden. Drain thoroughly and keep warm while frying the remainder.

Serves 4
Preparation time: *20 minutes*, plus
30 minutes standing time
Cooking time: about *20 minutes*

clipboard: Gram flour is ground garbanzo bean flour. It is excellent for making batter and is often used in India instead of wheat flour.

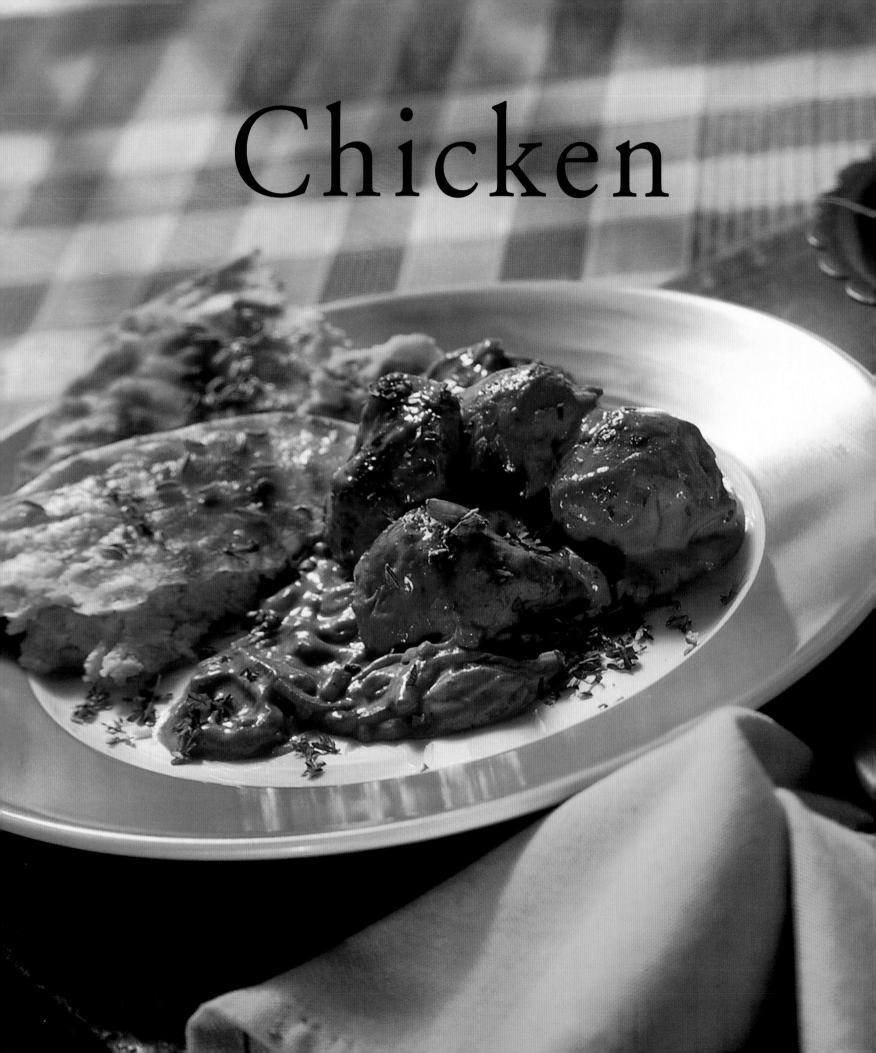

Chicken

Chicken Biriyani

8 chicken legs
¾ cup ghee or 5 tablespoons vegetable oil
2 tablespoons chopped almonds
2 tablespoons chopped cashews
1 large onion, finely chopped
4 bay leaves
1¾ cups long-grain rice
3¾ cups warm water
½ teaspoon saffron strands (optional)
2 tablespoons melted butter
salt
1 small red chile, finely sliced, to garnish
cilantro leaves, to garnish

Paste

1 teaspoon garam masala
1 small onion, chopped
2 garlic cloves, minced
2-inch piece of fresh ginger root
⅝ cup plain yogurt
1 teaspoon salt

Biriyani spices

4 cloves
8 black peppercorns
4 green cardamoms
1 black cardamom, crushed
2-inch piece of cinnamon stick
½ teaspoon turmeric

grind all the paste ingredients together in a mortar or food processor to make a smooth mixture. Rub this paste over the chicken legs and leave them to marinate for 30 minutes.

heat the ghee or oil in a skillet and fry the almonds and cashews until golden brown. Remove with a slotted spoon and drain on paper towels. Set aside for the garnish. Add the onion to the skillet and fry until golden. Remove half of the onion and keep for the garnish.

mix together the biriyani spices without grinding. Add them with the bay leaves to the onion in the skillet, stir well, and then add the chicken. Cook over a moderate heat for 20 minutes. Stir in the rice and then add the warm water and some salt. Cover and cook for 15–20 minutes, until the rice is tender and all the water absorbed.

soak the saffron in a little water for 5 minutes, if using. Add the melted butter and stir into the rice. Serve garnished with the reserved fried onions and nuts, chile slices, and cilantro leaves.

Serves 4
Preparation time: *30 minutes*, plus
    30 minutes marinating time
Cooking time: *50 minutes*

clipboard: Saffron is made from the dried stamens of a species of crocus. Over 4,000 blooms are required to yield 1 ounce of saffron, which is why it is the most expensive and highly prized of all the spices. It is available either as whole threads or ground into a powder. It is better to buy threads than powder, as the latter is easily adulterated, especially in the Far East where marigold or safflower stamens are often substituted for the real thing.

Chicken Korma

This mild curry, in which yogurt makes a delicately creamy sauce, is a favorite with many people who do not care for anything too hot or spicy.

¾ cup plain yogurt

2 teaspoons turmeric

3 garlic cloves, sliced

1 x 3-pound roasting chicken, skinned and cut into 8 pieces

½ cup ghee or 4 tablespoons vegetable oil

1 large onion, sliced

1 teaspoon ground ginger

2-inch piece of cinnamon stick

5 cloves

5 cardamom pods

1 tablespoon crushed coriander seeds

1 teaspoon ground cumin

½ teaspoon chili powder

1 teaspoon salt

1½ tablespoons desiccated coconut

2 teaspoons toasted almonds, to garnish

cilantro leaves, to garnish

put the yogurt, turmeric, and one of the garlic cloves in a blender or food processor and blend to a smooth purée.

place the chicken pieces in a shallow dish and pour the yogurt mixture over them. Cover the dish and leave to marinate in the refrigerator overnight.

heat the ghee or oil in a large, heavy-bottom saucepan and add the onion and remaining garlic. Cook gently for 4–5 minutes until soft. Add the spices and salt and fry for a further 3 minutes, stirring constantly.

add the chicken pieces with the yogurt marinade and coconut and mix well. Cover the pan with a tightly fitting lid and then simmer gently for 45 minutes, or until the chicken is cooked and tender. Transfer to a warmed serving dish and sprinkle with the almonds and cilantro leaves.

Serves 4
Preparation time: *15 minutes*, plus overnight marinating time
Cooking time: *55 minutes*

Tandoori Chicken

8 chicken pieces
8 tablespoons lemon juice
2 teaspoons salt

Marinade
10 cloves
2 teaspoons coriander seeds
2 teaspoons cumin seeds
seeds of 10 cardamoms
2 onions, chopped
4 garlic cloves, chopped
3-inch piece of fresh ginger root, peeled and chopped
2 teaspoons chili powder
2 teaspoons freshly ground black pepper
1½ teaspoons turmeric
1½ cups plain yogurt
few drops of red food coloring (optional)

remove the skin from the chicken pieces and discard. Wash and dry the chicken and then score each piece several times with a sharp knife. Place in a large dish and sprinkle with the lemon juice and salt. Rub this mixture in well, then cover and leave in a cool place for 1 hour.

prepare the marinade while the chicken is standing: spread the cloves, coriander, cumin, and cardamom seeds on a cookie sheet and roast in a preheated oven at 400°F for 10–15 minutes. Remove and, when cool, grind them coarsely in a mortar.

put the onions, garlic, and ginger in a blender or food processor and sprinkle with the chili powder, black pepper, and turmeric. Add the yogurt and ground roasted spices and strain in the lemon juice from the chicken. Blend until smooth, adding some red food coloring if wished.

place the chicken pieces in a single layer in a large roasting pan and pour over the marinade. Cover the pan and leave in the refrigerator to marinate for at least 24 hours, turning occasionally. Cook in a preheated oven at 400°F for 20 minutes and then place under a hot broiler until crisp. Serve hot or cold.

Serves 8
Preparation time: *45 minutes*, plus
  1 hour standing time, plus
  24 hours marinating time
Cooking time: *30 minutes*
Oven temperature: 400°F

Chicken Vindaloo

A chicken vindaloo is a fiery curry, and strictly not for the fainthearted! If you're worried about it being too hot, reduce the quantity of vindaloo masala.

2 tablespoons vindaloo masala
2 teaspoons vinegar
3 teaspoons salt
1 x 3-pound chicken, cut into pieces
6 tablespoons mustard or vegetable oil
4 bay leaves
1 teaspoon green cardamom seeds
1 large onion, thinly sliced
2 teaspoons turmeric
1 teaspoon cayenne
10 garlic cloves, minced
½ ounce fresh ginger root, thinly sliced
2 tomatoes, skinned and quartered
⅝ cup tamarind or lemon juice
2 teaspoons desiccated coconut

put the vindaloo masala, vinegar, and 2 teaspoons of the salt in a bowl and then mix well to make a smooth paste.

wash and dry the chicken pieces and then score each piece several times with a sharp knife. Rub the paste all over them and leave in a cool place to marinate for 1 hour.

heat the mustard oil in a large saucepan and stir in the bay leaves and cardamom seeds. Add the onion and fry until light brown. Stir in the turmeric and cayenne and add the chicken pieces. Cook, stirring occasionally, for 15 minutes. Add the reserved salt, garlic, ginger, and tomatoes and cook for 10 minutes, stirring.

add the tamarind or lemon juice to the pan when the fat starts to separate. Stir well, cover, and simmer gently for about 25 minutes, or until the chicken is tender. Sprinkle with coconut and serve.

Serves 6
Preparation time: *15 minutes*, plus
1 hour marinating time
Cooking time: *55 minutes*

Chicken and Lentils

with spinach and tomatoes

2½ cups dried split peas or lentils (e.g. moong dhal)

5 cups water

¾ cup ghee or 5 tablespoons vegetable oil

2 large onions, sliced

4 garlic cloves, sliced

6 cloves

6 cardamoms

1½ teaspoons ground ginger

2 teaspoons garam masala

2½ teaspoons salt

1 x 3-pound roasting chicken, skinned, boned, and cut into 8 pieces

1 pound frozen whole-leaf spinach

4 large tomatoes, skinned and chopped

wash the split peas or lentils and then place in a large saucepan. Add the measured water and bring to the boil. Cover the pan, lower the heat, and simmer for 15 minutes.

heat the ghee or oil in a large, heavy-bottom saucepan, add the onions and garlic and fry for 4–5 minutes until soft. Add the spices and salt and fry for 3 minutes, stirring constantly. Add the chicken and brown on all sides, then remove and drain on paper towels.

add the spinach and tomatoes to the saucepan and fry gently over a low heat for 10 minutes stirring occasionally.

mash the peas or lentils in their cooking water and then stir them into the spinach mixture. Return the chicken to the pan, cover with a tightly fitting lid, and simmer gently for 45 minutes, or until the chicken is cooked and tender.

Serves 4
Preparation time: *30 minutes*
Cooking time: *1¼ hours*

Roast Chicken with Almonds

2 tablespoons oil
6 tablespoons ghee or 1½ tablespoons vegetable oil
3 onions, chopped
pinch of ground saffron
1¼ cups plain yogurt
1 tablespoon coriander seeds
1 teaspoon cumin seeds
8 cloves
6 cardamom pods
1 x 3-pound roasting chicken
¾ cup blanched slivered almonds
⅓ cup raisins
salt
freshly ground black pepper

heat the oil and two-thirds of the ghee or corn oil in a skillet and add the onions. Fry until golden brown. Mix in the saffron and yogurt and set aside to cool.

put the coriander and cumin seeds, salt and pepper, cloves and cardamoms in a mortar, and pound well. Rub this spice mixture all over the chicken and place in a roasting pan.

cook the chicken in a preheated oven at 375°F for about 1¼ hours, until the chicken is cooked and tender. After about 20 minutes, baste the chicken with the yogurt mixture and return to the oven. Keep basting the chicken at regular intervals.

heat the reserved ghee or sunflower oil in a skillet and, while the chicken is cooking, sauté the almonds until they start to turn golden brown. Add the raisins and stir well. Remove from the heat. Serve the chicken, topped with the almonds and raisins, with some plain boiled rice.

Serves 4–6
Preparation time: *20 minutes*
Cooking time: *1¼ hours*
Oven temperature: 375°F

Chicken Pilau

1½ cups Basmati rice

5 tablespoons ghee or vegetable oil

2-inch piece of cinnamon stick

8 cloves

6 cardamom seeds

2 garlic cloves, minced

1 teaspoon chili powder

1 tablespoon fennel seeds

4 chicken pieces, skinned

5 tablespoons plain yogurt

1 teaspoon ground saffron

1½ teaspoons salt

2½ cups Chicken Stock (see page 11)

To garnish

2 large onions, sliced

4 tablespoons ghee

fresh cilantro leaves

wash the rice thoroughly and drain. Place in a large bowl and cover with fresh cold water. Let soak for 30 minutes and then drain well.

heat the ghee or oil in a large saucepan and add the cinnamon, cloves, and cardamom seeds. Cook briskly for 30 seconds and then stir in the garlic, chili powder, and fennel seeds. Cook for a further 30 seconds.

add the chicken pieces and cook, turning occasionally, for 5 minutes. Stir in the yogurt, a spoonful at a time, and then cover the pan and simmer for 25 minutes.

add the rice, saffron, and salt. Cook, stirring, until the rice is glistening and coated with spices. Add enough stock to cover the rice by ¼ inch and bring to the boil. Reduce the heat to a bare simmer and cook, covered tightly, for 20 minutes, or until the rice is cooked.

fry the onions in the ghee or oil in another pan. Use to garnish the pilau with the cilantro leaves.

Serves 4
Preparation time: *20 minutes*, plus
 30 minutes soaking time
Cooking time: *1–1¼ hours*

clipboard: Wild fennel has large, long, light greenish-brown seeds which have a slight aniseed flavour. They are much used in Indian cookery with meat, fish and vegetables, and are also used in spice mixtures. Whole roasted fennel seeds are also chewed in India after a meal, when they are said to have a digestive effect.

Chicken Tikka

Pieces of chicken marinated in yogurt flavored with ginger, cloves, chili powder, coriander seeds, and lemon juice make for a delicately spiced combination.

⅝ cup plain yogurt
1 tablespoon grated fresh ginger root
2 garlic cloves, minced
1 teaspoon chili powder
1 tablespoon ground coriander seeds
½ teaspoon salt
4 tablespoons lemon juice
2 tablespoons oil
1½ pounds chicken breasts, skinned, boned, and cubed

To garnish
1 onion, sliced
2 tomatoes, quartered
4 lemon twists

mix together in a bowl all the ingredients except the chicken. Drop the chicken cubes into the marinade. Cover and leave in the refrigerator overnight.

thread the chicken on to 4 skewers and cook under a preheated hot broiler for 5–6 minutes, turning frequently.

remove the chicken from the skewers and arrange on individual serving plates. Garnish with onion, tomato, and lemon to serve.

Serves 4
Preparation time: *15 minutes*, plus
    overnight marinating time
Cooking time: *5–6 minutes*

clipboard: The principal purpose of a marinade is to flavor food, but it also makes certain meats more tender by softening the fibers.

Chicken Tikka Masala

Chicken Tikka (see page 78), marinated and threaded on to skewers but not cooked
2 tablespoons chopped fresh cilantro leaves
juice of ½ lime

Masala sauce
4 tablespoons ghee or vegetable oil
2 onions, thinly sliced
1-inch piece of fresh ginger root, finely chopped
2 garlic cloves, minced
6 cardamoms, bruised
2 teaspoons garam masala
2 teaspoons ground coriander
1 teaspoon chili powder, or to taste
1¼ cups heavy cream
2 tablespoons tomato paste
4 tablespoons hot water
½ teaspoon sugar
½ teaspoon salt

To garnish
fresh cilantro leaves
slices of lime

make the masala sauce by heating the ghee or vegetable oil in a large flameproof casserole dish; add the onions, ginger, and garlic and cook over a gentle heat, stirring frequently, for about 5 minutes, until softened but not colored.

add the spices and fry, stirring, for 1–2 minutes, until fragrant, then add the cream, tomato paste, water, sugar, and salt. Bring slowly to the boil over a moderate heat, stirring, then lower the heat, and simmer gently, stirring occasionally, for 10–15 minutes. Remove the pan from the heat and let stand while cooking the chicken.

barbecue or broil the Chicken Tikka according to the recipe instructions on page 78, and then remove the cubes of chicken from the skewers.

tip the chicken into the masala sauce, return to a low heat and simmer, stirring, for about 5 minutes. Add the chopped cilantro leaves and lime juice, and taste for seasoning. Serve immediately, garnished with cilantro leaves and slices of lime and accompanied by plain boiled rice, chapatis, or naan bread.

Serves 4
Preparation time: *20 minutes*
Cooking time: *40–45 minutes*

clipboard: The aroma of the cardamom is contained within the seeds—small black seeds within a papery pod. Cardamom is related to ginger and is widely grown in the tropical regions of India.

Kashmiri Chicken

The addition of plain yogurt toward the end of the cooking time gives this a deliciously mild and creamy flavor, which makes a wonderful contrast to all the spices.

4 tablespoons ghee or vegeetable oil

3 large onions, finely sliced

10 peppercorns

10 cardamoms

2-inch piece of cinnamon stick

2-inch piece of fresh ginger root, chopped

2 garlic cloves, finely chopped

1 teaspoon chili powder

2 teaspoons paprika

3 pounds chicken pieces, skinned

1 cup plain yogurt

salt

heat the ghee or vegetable oil in a deep, lidded skillet. Add the onions, peppercorns, cardamoms, and cinnamon and cook until the onions are golden. Add the ginger, garlic, chili powder, paprika, and salt to taste and cook for 2 minutes, stirring occasionally.

add the chicken pieces and fry until browned. Gradually add the yogurt, stirring constantly. Cover and cook gently for about 30 minutes.

Serves 6
Preparation time: *20 minutes*
Cooking time: *30–35 minutes*

clipboard: Paprika is made from mild varieties of capsicum, or sweet pepper, which have had their seeds and inner membranes removed before being dried and ground. It should be bought in small quantities and replaced often, as its flavor and color both deteriorate rapidly. It should be a bright red color, which shows that it is fresh.

Palak Murg

This mild chicken dish is both quick and simple to make, and the combination of chicken with ginger, coriander seeds, and chili powder is a highly successful one.

3 tablespoons oil
2 onions, chopped
2 garlic cloves, minced
1-inch piece of fresh ginger root, chopped
2 teaspoons ground coriander seeds
1 teaspoon chili powder
1½ pounds chicken legs and thighs, skinned
1½ pounds fresh spinach, washed and trimmed
milk (optional)
salt

heat the oil in a large saucepan, add the onions and cook until golden. Add the garlic, ginger, coriander, chili powder, and salt to taste and cook gently for 2 minutes, stirring.

add the chicken and fry on all sides until browned. Add the spinach, stir well, cover, and simmer for 35 minutes, until the chicken is tender.

stir in 2–3 tablespoons milk if the mixture becomes too dry during cooking. If there is too much liquid left at the end, uncover and cook for a few minutes until it has evaporated.

Serves 4
Preparation time: *20 minutes*
Cooking time: *35–40 minutes*

clipboard: Fresh ginger root is often required in Indian cooking. It freezes very well—simply wrap it in plastic wrap or in a small freezer bag. You can then use exactly the amount you need, and return the rest to the freezer for use later. Ginger can also be kept in the refrigerator in a tightly sealed jar of dry sherry. Ground ginger is not an acceptable substitute for the real thing.

Chicken Molee

with ginger and creamed coconut

about 3 tablespoons oil

4 chicken breasts, skinned, boned, and cut into 3–4 pieces

6 cardamoms

6 cloves

2-inch piece of cinnamon stick

I large onion, finely sliced

2 garlic cloves

1½-inch piece of fresh ginger root, chopped

3 fresh green chiles, seeded

4 tablespoons lemon juice

I teaspoon turmeric

2 ounces creamed coconut

⅝ cup hot water

salt

heat the oil in a pan, add the chicken, and fry quickly all over. Remove with a slotted spoon and set aside.

add a little more oil to the pan if necessary and fry the cardamoms, cloves, and cinnamon for 1 minute. Add the onion and fry until soft.

place the garlic, ginger, chiles, and lemon juice in a blender or food processor and work to a smooth paste. Add to the pan with the turmeric and cook for 5 minutes.

melt the coconut in the hot water and add to the pan with salt to taste. Simmer for 2 minutes, then add the chicken pieces and any juices. Simmer for 15–20 minutes, until tender.

Serves 4
Preparation time: *25 minutes*
Cooking time: *25–30 minutes*

clipboard: Cinnamon is the thinly rolled inner bark of an evergreen tree that grows abundantly in southern India. It is often used in India to flavor meat and rice dishes, and is one of the ingredients in commercially manufactured curry powder.

Chicken Makhani

Tomatoes and butter are the characteristic ingredients of a makhani, a refined and elegant dish. Naan bread is a good accompaniment.

1½ pounds skinned, boned chicken breasts or thighs, cut into 2-inch pieces

3 tablespoons vegetable oil

Marinade

3 large fresh red chiles, seeded and chopped

4 garlic cloves, minced

2 teaspoons toasted cumin seeds, crushed

1 teaspoon garam masala

½ teaspoon salt

2 tablespoons fresh cilantro leaves

4 tablespoons lemon juice

⅝ cup plain yogurt

Sauce

3 pounds ripe tomatoes, quartered

4 tablespoons butter

⅝ cup heavy cream

salt

To garnish

1 tablespoon heavy cream

sprigs of fresh cilantro

Serves 6
Preparation time: *15 minutes*, plus
  3 hours marinating time
Cooking time: *2¼ hours*

start by making the marinade. Place the chiles, garlic, and cumin seeds in a blender or food processor and blend briefly before adding the remaining ingredients and blending to produce a paste.

transfer the marinade to a non-metallic bowl. Add the chicken to the marinade, turning to coat them evenly. Cover and refrigerate for 3 hours.

prepare the sauce while the chicken is marinating. Put the tomatoes in a large saucepan and cook them gently, with no added water, for about 20 minutes, or until they are tender. Then rub them through a fine strainer into a clean saucepan. Simmer the tomato pulp, stirring occasionally, for about 50 minutes, until it is thick and reduced.

stir in the butter and a little salt and cook the sauce over a medium heat, stirring often, for a further 30 minutes, until it is thick. Stir in the cream and heat it through. Taste and adjust the amount of salt if necessary and set the sauce aside.

heat the oil in a large heavy-bottomed sauté pan. Remove the chicken pieces from their marinade, reserving the marinade, and fry gently to seal them, for about 5 minutes. Add the marinade to the pan, increase the heat and cook, stirring frequently, for a further 12 minutes, or until the chicken is cooked through.

reduce the heat and pour the tomato sauce over the chicken. Simmer gently for a further 5 minutes. Transfer the chicken to a serving dish and garnish with a swirl of cream and a few cilantro sprigs.

Bangalore Chicken Curry

This "green" curry from central southern India is made with a lot of fresh cilantro and fresh green chiles.

3 tablespoons ghee or vegetable oil

2 onions, thinly sliced

6 garlic cloves, chopped

1 teaspoon turmeric

1½ teaspoons ground dhana jeera (¾ teaspoon ground coriander and ¾ teaspoon ground cumin)

1½ ounces fresh cilantro leaves

3 large fresh green chiles, seeded and chopped

1 x 3½-pound chicken, cut into 8 pieces

⅝ cup Chicken Stock (see page 11)

1¼ cups unsweetened coconut milk

1 teaspoon salt

1 tablespoon lemon juice

fresh cilantro leaves, to garnish

heat the ghee or oil in a large heavy-bottom skillet. Add the onions and fry over a medium heat, stirring frequently, for about 5 minutes, or until they are softened and golden.

stir in the garlic, turmeric, and dhana jeera and cook, stirring, for a further 3 minutes.

place the cilantro leaves and green chiles in a blender or food processor and blend to a paste. Add this paste to the skillet, reduce the heat to very low, and cook, stirring constantly, for a further 10 minutes.

add the chicken pieces to the skillet, turn them in the spice mixture to coat them evenly, then add the stock, coconut milk, and salt. Bring to the boil, then reduce the heat, cover, and simmer, stirring and turning the chicken occasionally, for about 50 minutes, or until the juices from the chicken run clear when tested with a skewer. Stir in the lemon juice and taste and adjust the amount of salt if necessary.

transfer the cooked chicken pieces to a serving dish and keep them warm. Increase the heat and boil the curry sauce for 5–8 minutes to thicken it. Pour it over the chicken and garnish with cilantro.

Serves 6
Preparation time: *20 minutes*
Cooking time: *1 hour 20 minutes*

Balti Chicken

with green pepper

6 tablespoons oil

I onion, chopped

½ teaspoon ground turmeric

I teaspoon ground coriander

I teaspoon ground cumin

I teaspoon chili powder

2 tablespoons water

1½ pounds skinned, boned chicken, cubed

3 cups chopped tomatoes

I large green bell pepper, seeded and cut into squares

4–6 garlic cloves, chopped

2 fresh green chiles, chopped

salt

To garnish

2 tomatoes, quartered

sprigs of fresh cilantro

heat the oil in a large wok or heavy-bottom saucepan, add the onion and cook until soft. Mix the turmeric, coriander, cumin, and chili powder with the water. Stir this spice mixture into the onion and cook until the liquid has evaporated, about 3–4 minutes.

add the chicken and fry on all sides, then add the tomatoes and a pinch of salt to taste. Cover and cook for 15 minutes.

stir in the green bell pepper, garlic, and chiles. Cook, uncovered, until all the tomato juices have evaporated and the chicken is cooked through. Serve hot, garnished with the tomatoes and sprigs of cilantro.

Serves 4–6
Preparation time: *20 minutes*
Cooking time: *30–40 minutes*

clipboard: Garlic should be stored in a cool place, either laid out flat or hanging in bunches to improve aeration. Generally speaking, white garlic lasts about 6 months, and pink garlic nearly a year.

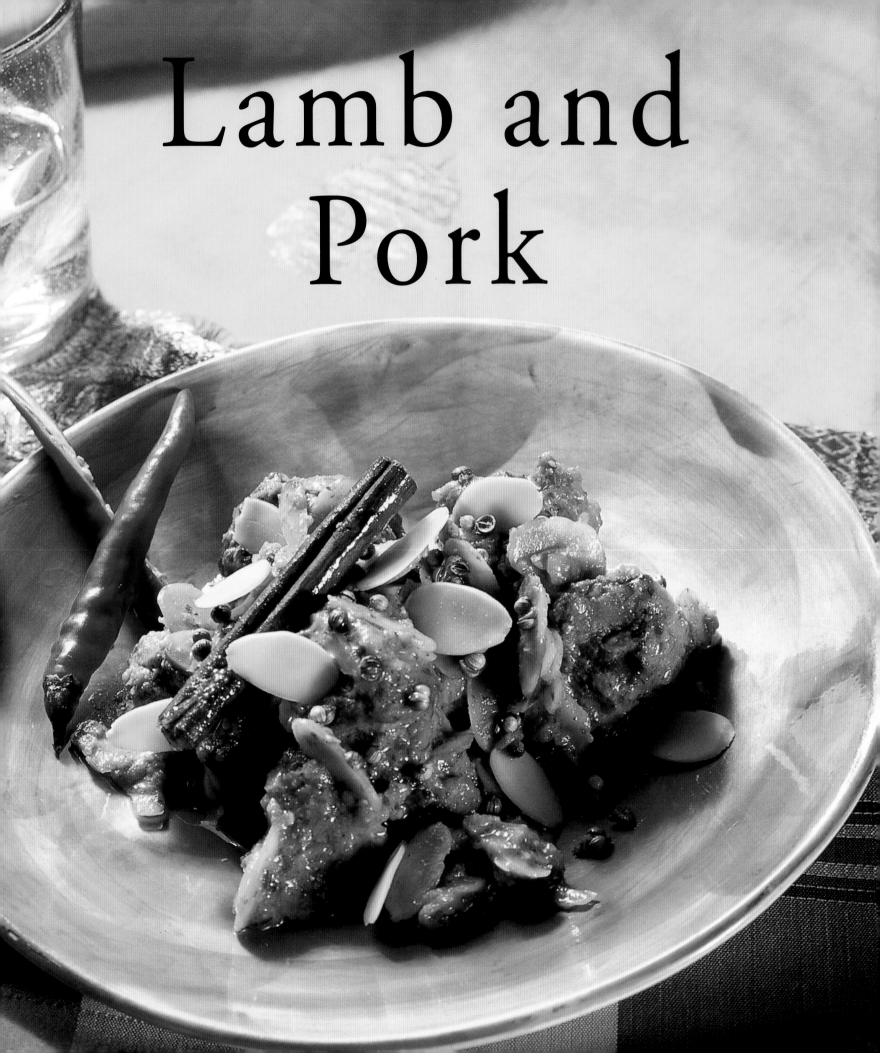

Lamb and Pork

Lamb Kebobs

Ground lamb is made into a sausage with spices and lemon juice, and the "sausages" are then threaded on to skewers and grilled.

3 cups ground lean lamb

1 teaspoon grated fresh ginger root

1 large onion, finely chopped

3–4 tablespoons garbanzo bean or gram flour (besan)

2 fresh green chiles, finely chopped

1 teaspoon green mango powder

1 tablespoon salt

2 tablespoons lemon juice

1 egg

2 tablespoons chopped fresh cilantro leaves

¼ cup melted ghee or 1 tablespoon vegetable oil

lime wedges, to garnish

Spices

½ teaspoon poppy seeds, roasted and ground

1 teaspoon garam masala

1 tablespoon yellow or red chili powder

½ teaspoon freshly ground black pepper

1 teaspoon black cumin seeds, roasted and ground

1 tablespoon ground coriander seeds

mix the ground meat, ginger, onion, garbanzo or gram flour, chiles, mango powder, salt, and lemon juice together with all the spices. Set aside for 30 minutes to allow the flavors to develop.

work the egg and chopped cilantro into the ground meat mixture. Continue kneading the mixture until it becomes sticky.

divide the ground meat mixture into 18 equal-sized portions and then form each piece between your hands into a sausage shape.

thread the "sausages" on to skewers. For longer kebobs, flatten them out on the skewers. Cook under a preheated hot broiler or over a charcoal grill, turning frequently. Brush the kebobs with melted ghee or oil while they are cooking. Serve hot, garnished with lime wedges.

Serves 6
Preparation time: *30 minutes*, plus
  30 minutes standing time
Cooking time: *20–30 minutes*

clipboard: Mango powder, also known as aamchoor, is a sour-tasting powder made from raw mangoes. It is sold in jars in specialist Indian food stores.

Lamb with Almonds

¼ cup ghee or 1 tablespoon vegetable oil
½ cup finely chopped onion
5 small green cardamoms
½ teaspoon ground turmeric
1 teaspoon chili powder
1 teaspoon ground cumin
1½ teaspoons paprika
1 teaspoon ground coriander
⅝ cup plain yogurt
8 ounces tomatoes, skinned and chopped
1 pound lean lamb, cut into 1-inch cubes
salt
chopped fresh cilantro leaves, to garnish

Masala

½ ounce fresh ginger root, peeled and chopped
6 garlic cloves, peeled
1 blade of mace
¼ teaspoon ground nutmeg
4 cloves
1 tablespoon dry roasted poppy seeds
12 peppercorns
½ cup blanched almonds
seeds of 2 large cardamoms

make the masala first: grind the ginger, garlic, mace, nutmeg, cloves, poppy seeds, peppercorns, almonds, and cardamom seeds. Add a little water to make a fine paste.

heat the ghee or oil in a deep skillet and gently fry the onion until light brown. Add the small green cardamoms and stir in the masala paste. Fry over a low heat for 2 minutes.

add the turmeric, chili powder, cumin, paprika, and coriander to the skillet, and cook over a gentle heat for a further 1–2 minutes.

stir in the yogurt and tomatoes and then the lamb with a little salt. Cover and cook over a low heat for 40–50 minutes, sprinkling with a little water if necessary. Serve garnished with cilantro.

Serves 4
Preparation time: *30 minutes*
Cooking time: *1¼ hours*

clipboard: Yogurt is often used in Indian cooking to add a sharp creaminess. Use a plain yogurt—preferably a thin acidic-flavored variety rather then a milder, creamier type. If you use a "set" yogurt, always stir it a little to break up the "setting" before adding it to the dish.

Kheema do Pyaza

Ground lamb is delicately spiced and then simmered with plain yogurt and tomatoes until the meat is cooked— an unusual combination.

1 pound onions
4 tablespoons oil
1-inch piece of fresh ginger root, chopped
1 garlic clove, finely chopped
2 fresh green chiles, finely chopped
1 teaspoon turmeric
1 teaspoon ground coriander seeds
1 teaspoon ground cumin seeds
3 cups ground lamb
⅝ cup plain yogurt
1 x 8-ounce can tomatoes
salt

chop 12 ounces of the onions finely; thinly slice the remainder.

measure 2 tablespoons of the oil into a pan, add the chopped onion and cook until golden. Add the ginger, garlic, chiles, and spices and fry for 2 minutes. Add the ground lamb and cook, stirring to break up, until well browned.

stir in the yogurt, spoon by spoon, until it is absorbed, then add the tomatoes with their juice and salt to taste. Bring to the boil, stir well, cover, and simmer for 20 minutes, or until the meat is cooked.

heat the remaining oil while the lamb is cooking and fry the sliced onions until brown and crisp. Transfer the meat mixture to a warmed serving dish and sprinkle with the fried onion.

Serves 4
Preparation time: *30 minutes*
Cooking time: *30–40 minutes*

Roghan Ghosht

This unusual combination of cubed lamb cooked gently in mildly spiced yogurt with chopped fresh mint leaves and slivered almonds is absolutely delicious.

4 tablespoons oil

2 onions, finely chopped

1½ pounds lean lamb, cubed

1¼ cups plain yogurt

2 garlic cloves, peeled

1-inch piece of fresh ginger root

2 fresh green chiles

1 tablespoon coriander seeds

1 teaspoon cumin seeds

1 teaspoon chopped fresh mint leaves

1 teaspoon chopped fresh cilantro leaves

6 cardamoms

6 cloves

1-inch piece of cinnamon stick

1 cup slivered almonds

salt

heat 2 tablespoons of the oil in a pan, add half of the onions, and fry until golden. Add the lamb and half of the yogurt, stir well, cover, and simmer for 20 minutes.

place the garlic, ginger, chiles, coriander seeds, cumin seeds, mint, fresh cilantro, and 2–3 tablespoons yogurt in a blender or food processor and blend to a paste.

take a large saucepan and heat the remaining oil, add the cardamoms, cloves, and cinnamon and cook for 1 minute, stirring. Add the remaining onion and the prepared paste and cook for 5 minutes, stirring constantly.

add the lamb and yogurt mixture, and salt to taste, stir well and bring to simmering point. Cover and cook for 30 minutes. Add the almonds and cook for a further 15 minutes, until the meat is tender.

Serves 4
Preparation time: *30 minutes*
Cooking time: *1 hour 15 minutes*

Utensils

Turning bowl

Ladle

Measuring jug

Turning bowl

A turning bowl is a useful piece of equipment. It is used for mixing, beating, or folding mixtures. It has a built-in stand to support it and to stop it slipping while you work. It can be used for working at different angles. The stainless steel surface is not only durable but also very easy to keep clean.

Measuring jug

A measuring jug is a standardized measure of liquid. It has a handle and a good pouring lip. It is usually marked with both pints and cup measures. It is available in glass, plastic, or stainless steel. It is always advisable to check before purchasing a jug that it is dishwasher safe.

Whisk

A whisk is an essential beating tool, which is used to blend ingredients and to incorporate air into batters or cake mixtures. Whisks come in a variety of different shapes and sizes: small ones are used for sauces, while the larger balloon whisk is the most popular and commonly used. A whisk is useful, too, for rescuing a lumpy sauce.

Ladle

A ladle is used as a serving utensil. A deep, long-handled spoon, it is usually used to transfer a soup or stew from the pan to the serving dish. It is usually made of stainless steel, which is durable and easy to keep clean.

Whisk

Large skillet

Flat skillet

Skimmer

Turner

Large skillet
The best skillet is made of a strong, heat-conducting metal, which allows heat to be transmitted rapidly and evenly. It should have a wide, flat bottom and shallow sides, sloping outward to give space for lifting and turning food. A long handle means that it is easy to lift.

Turner
A turner is an indispensable piece of kitchen equipment, which will be useful on a daily basis. It is a wide-blade implement, which is used to lift, turn, and transfer food—such as slices of bacon, fried eggs, pieces of meat or fillets of fish—from the pan or cookie sheet to the serving dish. It is usually made of stainless steel, as it is both strong, durable, and easy to maintain, and will last you for many years.

Skimmer
A skimmer is a shallow, long-handled spoon, which is perforated all over in order that food may be removed from a pan and, in the process, any unwanted liquid will simply drain away. Skimmers are usually made of stainless steel.

Flat skillet
You also need a flat, wide skillet, which is used for rapid cooking purposes on top of the cooker. It can be used either to fry food, or to make sauces. A skillet should be an efficient heat conductor and often has a nonstick finish.

Lamb Korma

Mild and creamy, lamb korma is made with cubed leg of lamb, lightly spiced with a subtle combination of spices and cooked in creamy plain yogurt.

5 tablespoons oil

6 cardamoms

6 cloves

6 peppercorns

1-inch piece of cinnamon stick

1½ pounds lean lamb, cubed

6 shallots or 1 small onion, chopped

2 garlic cloves, finely chopped

2-inch piece of fresh ginger root, chopped

2 tablespoons ground coriander seeds

2 teaspoons ground cumin seeds

1 teaspoon chili powder

⅝ cup plain yogurt

1 teaspoon garam masala

salt

2 tablespoons finely chopped fresh cilantro leaves, to garnish (optional)

heat 4 tablespoons of the oil in a saucepan, add the cardamoms, cloves, peppercorns, and cinnamon and fry for 1 minute.

add the lamb, a few pieces at a time, and fry well to brown all over; transfer to a dish. Remove the whole spices and discard.

add the remaining oil to the pan and fry the shallots (or onion), garlic, and ginger for 5 minutes, then add the coriander and cumin seeds, chili powder, and salt to taste and cook for 5 minutes, stirring to avoid burning. Gradually stir in the yogurt until it is all absorbed.

return the meat to the pan with any liquid collected in the dish and add sufficient water just to cover the meat. Bring to simmering point, cover, and cook for about 1 hour, or until the meat is tender.

sprinkle on the garam masala and cook, stirring, for 1 minute. Garnish with chopped cilantro, if liked, before serving.

Serves 4
Preparation time: *25 minutes*
Cooking time: *1½ hours*

Raan

5 pounds lean lamb, skin and fat removed
2 ounces fresh ginger root, chopped
6 garlic cloves, peeled
rind of 1 lemon
8 tablespoons lemon juice
2 teaspoons cumin seeds
6 cardamoms, peeled
1 teaspoon ground cloves
1 teaspoon turmeric
1½ teaspoons chili powder
1 tablespoon salt
1¼ cups plain yogurt
1 cup whole unpeeled almonds
4 tablespoons brown sugar
1 teaspoon saffron threads, soaked in 3 tablespoons boiling water
flatleaf parsley, to garnish

prick the lamb all over with a fork and make about 12 deep cuts.

blend the ginger, garlic, lemon rind and juice, spices, and salt in a blender or food processor. Spread over the lamb and let stand for 1 hour in a flameproof casserole dish.

combine 4 tablespoons of the yogurt with the almonds and 2 tablespoons of the sugar. Stir in the remaining yogurt and and pour over the lamb. Cover tightly and leave for 48 hours in the refrigerator.

allow the meat to return to room temperature. Sprinkle over the remaining sugar and cook, uncovered, in a preheated hot oven at 425°F for 30 minutes. Cover, lower the temperature to 325°F and cook for 3 hours, basting occasionally. Sprinkle the saffron water over the meat and cook for a further 30 minutes, or until very tender.

remove the meat from the casserole dish, wrap it in foil, and keep warm. Skim off the fat from the casserole and boil the sauce until thick. Place the meat on a dish and pour over the sauce. Carve in thick slices to serve and garnish with parsley sprigs.

Serves 6
Preparation time: *20 minutes*, plus 1 hour
  standing time, plus 48 hours marinating time
Cooking time: *about 4 hours*
Oven temperature: 425°F, then 325°F

clipboard: Cloves are the immature, unopened flowerbuds of an evergreen tree that grows near the coast of tropical areas of southeast Asia, east Africa, and the West Indies. They can be bought whole or ground, and are often used in India in meat and rice dishes.

Lamb Dhansak

Dhansak is a Parsee dish from western India, traditionally served on special occasions.

⅓ cup each red lentils, garbanzo beans, and moong dhal
1½ pounds lean lamb fillet, cut into 2-inch cubes
10 ounces eggplant, cubed
8 ounces pumpkin, peeled and cubed
4 ounces potato, peeled and cubed
2 onions, coarsely chopped
2 tomatoes, skinned and chopped
3 ounces fresh spinach, washed
3 tablespoons ghee or oil
1 large onion, thinly sliced
2 tablespoons tomato paste
salt
freshly ground black pepper
deep-fried onion slices, to garnish

Masala mixture
3 fresh red chiles, seeded and chopped
3 fresh green chiles, seeded and chopped
6 garlic cloves, minced
1-inch piece of fresh ginger root, finely chopped
1 ounce fresh cilantro leaves
½ ounce fresh mint leaves
4 tablespoons water

Dry spice mixture
2 teaspoons turmeric
1 teaspoon black mustard seeds
½ teaspoon ground cinnamon
¼ teaspoon fenugreek powder
2 tablespoons dhana jeera powder
4 cardamoms, crushed

wash the lentils, garbanzos, and moong dhal. Soak overnight in cold water.

drain the legumes the next day, and place in a large saucepan with the lamb. Pour over enough boiling water to cover the legumes and meat and season generously with salt. Bring to the boil, skim any scum from the surface, then cover and simmer, stirring occasionally, for about 20 minutes.

tip all the prepared vegetables into the pan, stir and continue cooking for a further 40 minutes, until the legumes and vegetables are cooked and the lamb is tender. Drain the liquid from the pan and remove the pieces of meat with a slotted spoon. Set the meat aside and tip the vegetables and legumes into a blender or food processor. Blend to a thick purée.

heat the ghee or oil in a large heavy-bottom skillet and sauté the onion over a gentle heat for 5 minutes, until it is softened and golden.

place all the masala ingredients in a food processor and blend to a paste. Add this paste to the softened onion and cook gently for a further 3 minutes. Stir in the dry spice mixture and cook, stirring, for 3 minutes.

add the lamb and vegetable purée to the skillet, with the tomato paste and water. Season, cover, and simmer for 30 minutes, until thick. If it gets too dry, add a little more water. Taste and adjust seasoning if necessary.

transfer to serving dish, garnish with fried onions and serve with rice.

Serves 6
Preparation time: *30 minutes*, plus overnight soaking time
Cooking time: *1¾ hours*

Balti Lamb Madras

with tomatoes and coconut flakes

1 tablespoon oil
1 onion, chopped
2 garlic cloves, minced
2 fresh green chiles, seeded and sliced
2 teaspoons chili powder
2 teaspoons garam masala
1 pound lean lamb, cut into 1½-inch cubes
1 tablespoon vinegar
1 teaspoon salt
2 tomatoes, skinned, seeded, and chopped
1 tablespoon coconut flakes, to garnish

heat the oil in a wok or heavy-bottom skillet and stir-fry the onion, garlic, chiles, and chili powder for 2 minutes. Add the garam masala, lamb, vinegar, salt, and chopped tomatoes. Stir the mixture thoroughly.

cover the wok and cook for 30–40 minutes over a moderate heat until the lamb is tender, adding a little water if it appears to be sticking to the bottom of the wok.

transfer to a heated serving dish, scatter with the coconut flakes and serve immediately.

Serves 4
Preparation time: *10 minutes*
Cooking time: *35–45 minutes*

clipboard: Garam masala is a speciality from northern India, and varies from one region to another. It is generally a mild, sweet seasoning, and is available in many food markets and gourmet food stores. The mixture usually consists of cardamom, cinnamon, cloves, cumin, coriander, and black peppercorns. Optional extras may include nutmeg, mace, and bay leaves.

Pork Vindaloo

This powerful pork curry is just the thing for devoted fans of spicy food. It owes some of its kick to a combination of spices, including mustard seeds, and to the addition of vinegar.

1–2 teaspoons chili powder
1 teaspoon turmeric
2 teaspoons ground cumin seeds
2 teaspoons ground mustard seeds
2 tablespoons ground coriander seeds
1½-inch piece of fresh ginger root, finely chopped
⅝ cup vinegar
1 large onion, finely chopped
2 garlic cloves, minced
1½ pounds lean pork fillet, cubed
4 tablespoons oil
salt

mix the spices, and salt to taste, with the vinegar. Put the onion, garlic, and pork in a bowl, pour over the vinegar mixture, cover and leave in the refrigerator overnight.

heat the oil in a large saucepan, add the pork mixture, bring to simmering point, cover, and cook for about 45 minutes, or until the pork is tender.

Serves 4
Preparation time: *10 minutes*, plus overnight marinating time
Cooking time: *55 minutes*

clipboard: Black and brown mustard is a native of India and is often used in Indian cooking—either in the form of whole seeds, which are heated in oil until they splutter at the start of the cooking, or ground, as in this recipe.

Bhuna Ghosht

with coriander and lemon

1½ pounds pork fillets
2 tablespoons coriander seeds, coarsely pounded
1 teaspoon freshly ground black pepper
1 tablespoon paprika
4 tablespoons vegetable oil
salt
2 tablespoons finely chopped fresh cilantro leaves, to garnish
lemon wedges, to serve

slit the pork fillets lengthwise and cut each side into quarters. Prick the pieces all over with a fork. Mix together the coriander, pepper, paprika, and salt and rub into the meat on both sides. Let stand for 1 hour.

heat the oil in a pan, add the meat, and fry quickly on both sides to seal. Lower the heat and sauté for 5 minutes, or until cooked through, stirring and turning to prevent burning.

sprinkle with the chopped cilantro and serve with wedges of lemon.

Serves 4
Preparation time: *10 minutes*, plus
  1 hour standing time
Cooking time: *10 minutes*

clipboard: Coriander seeds can be coarsely pounded using a pestle and mortar, which consists of a bowl with a pounding tool. These are available in wood, ceramic, or marble, and the inner surface should be rough, not smooth.

Beef

Meatball Curry

2 cups ground beef

2 large onions, chopped

4 garlic cloves, minced

2 teaspoons turmeric

2 teaspoons chili powder

2 teaspoons ground coriander

1½ teaspoons ground cumin

1 teaspoon ground ginger

2 teaspoons salt

1 egg, beaten

oil for deep frying

½ cup ghee or 2 tablespoons vegetable oil

¾ cup water

mint or cilantro leaves, to garnish

put the ground beef in a bowl with half of the onions, garlic, spices, and salt. Stir well and then bind the mixture together with the beaten egg.

divide the ground beef mixture into 12 equal-sized portions and, using your hands, shape each one into a small ball.

heat the oil in a heavy-bottom saucepan until it is very hot. Add the meatballs in batches and deep fry for 5 minutes. Remove and drain on paper towels and then set aside and keep warm.

heat the ghee or oil in a large saucepan, add the remaining onions and garlic, and cook gently for 4–5 minutes, until soft. Add the remaining spices and salt and cook for 3 minutes, stirring constantly. Add the meatballs and coat them in the spices. Add the water and bring to the boil. Lower the heat and simmer gently for 30 minutes. Serve garnished with mint or cilantro leaves.

Serves 4
Preparation time: *30 minutes*
Cooking time: *40 minutes*

Calcutta Beef Curry

This beef curry is a rich and hearty dish and is unusual in that it is simmered for a long time in a mixture of milk and spices until the meat is tender and the sauce well reduced.

1 teaspoon salt

1 tablespoon chili powder

2 teaspoons ground coriander

1 teaspoon freshly ground black pepper

1½ teaspoons turmeric

1 teaspoon ground cumin

3¼ cups milk

2 pounds flank steak, trimmed of fat and cut into 1½-inch cubes

½ cup ghee or 2 tablespoons oil

2 large onions, thinly sliced

5 garlic cloves, thinly sliced

3-inch piece of fresh ginger root, peeled and thinly sliced

2 teaspoons garam masala

put the salt and ground spices, except the garam masala, in a large bowl. Mix in the milk, a little at a time.

add the cubes of beef to the bowl and turn in the milk and spice mixture until they are evenly coated.

heat the ghee or oil in a large, heavy-bottom saucepan, add the onions, garlic, and ginger and cook gently for 4–5 minutes until soft. Remove the cubes of beef from the milk and spice mixture and add to the saucepan. Cook gently over a moderate heat, turning constantly, until the meat is evenly browned.

increase the heat, add the milk and spice mixture and bring to the boil. Cover the pan, reduce the heat, and cook gently for 1½–2 hours, until the beef is tender and the sauce reduced. Just before serving, add the garam masala and boil off any excess liquid to make a thick sauce.

Serves 6
Preparation time: *15 minutes*
Cooking time: *1¾–2¼ hours*

Spicy Beef in Yogurt

Hot and spicy, this beef curry has some of the heat taken out of it by the yogurt. Marinating and slow cooking make it both tender and succulent.

1 pound round steak or stewing beef, finely sliced

1 teaspoon salt

1¼ cups plain yogurt

¾ cup ghee or 3 tablespoons oil

1 large onion, sliced

3 garlic cloves, sliced

1½ teaspoons ground ginger

2 teaspoons ground coriander

2 teaspoons chili powder

½ teaspoon ground cumin

1½ teaspoons turmeric

1 teaspoon garam masala

place the beef between 2 sheets of waxed paper and beat until thin with a rolling pin or mallet.

rub the beef with the salt and then cut into serving-sized pieces. Place in a bowl and cover with the yogurt. Cover and leave to marinate overnight in the refrigerator.

heat the ghee or oil in a heavy-bottom saucepan and add the onion and garlic. Cook gently for 4–5 minutes until soft. Add the spices and cook for a further 3 minutes, stirring constantly.

add the beef and yogurt marinade to the pan and stir well. Cover the pan with a tightly fitting lid and then simmer for 1½ hours, or until the meat is tender. Serve with rice.

Serves 4
Preparation time: *15 minutes*, plus
   overnight marinating time
Cooking time: *1¾ hours*

Beef Buffad

Cook cubed braising steak slowly with a subtle combination of spices and coconut milk until the meat is tender and succulent, and the sauce is rich and thick.

3 tablespoons vegetable oil
2 onions, sliced
2 garlic cloves, finely chopped
3 fresh green chiles, chopped
1½-inch piece of fresh ginger root, chopped
1½ pounds round steak, cubed
½ teaspoon chili powder
1 teaspoon turmeric
1 teaspoon freshly ground black pepper
1 teaspoon ground cumin seeds
1 tablespoon ground coriander seeds
½ teaspoon ground cinnamon
½ teaspoon ground cloves
1¼ cups coconut milk
⅝ cup vinegar
salt

heat the oil in a large saucepan, add the onions, and cook until they are just beginning to brown, then add the garlic, chiles, and ginger. Cook for 1 minute, then add the beef and remaining spices. Stir well and cook for 5 minutes, stirring occasionally.

add the coconut milk, which should just cover the meat; if it does not, add a little water. Add salt to taste. Bring to simmering point, cover and cook for about 1½ hours, until the meat is almost tender.

stir in the vinegar and continue cooking for about 30 minutes, until the meat is tender and the gravy is thick.

Serves 4
Preparation time: *30 minutes*
Cooking time: *2 hours*

clipboard: If you cannot find any coconut milk, you can use 3 ounces creamed coconut melted in 1 cup warm water instead. Creamed coconut is sold in blocks, which should always be softened in warm water before use.

Bell Peppers
stuffed with beef, rice, and tomatoes

5 tablespoons vegetable oil
1 onion, finely chopped
2 teaspoons ground coriander seeds
1 teaspoon ground cumin seeds
½ teaspoon chili powder
1½ cups ground beef
3 tablespoons long-grain rice
4 large green or red bell peppers
1 x 14-oz can tomatoes
salt

heat 3 tablespoons of the oil in a saucepan, add the onion, and cook until golden. Add the spices and cook for 2 minutes. Add the ground beef and fry, stirring, until browned. Add the rice and salt to taste and cook for 2 minutes. Remove from the heat and leave to cool.

slice the peppers lengthwise and discard the seeds and cores. Fill the pepper shells with the meat mixture.

pour the remaining oil into a pan just large enough to hold the peppers. Heat the oil and place the peppers in the pan. Pour a little of the canned tomato juice into each pepper and the remaining juice and tomatoes into the pan, seasoning with salt to taste. Bring to simmering point, cover, and cook for about 25 minutes until the rice is tender.

Serves 4
Preparation time: *35 minutes*
Cooking time: *30 minutes*

clipboard: A variation of this recipe using lamb instead of beef is also delicious, especially if you use succulent spring lamb.

Rice, grains and pulses

Garbanzo beans

Brown Basmati rice

Whole-wheat flour

Sprouted mung bean

Garbanzo beans
These are small pea-shaped seeds, which are pale golden in color and have a pleasantly nutty flavor. They are often used in stews or soups, and are also boiled and ground to a paste to make hummus. Garbanzos are used to make a special flour, known as besan. This is a very fine yellow flour used in bread cookery. The garbanzos are ground very finely. The flour should be sifted before use as it tends to form hard lumps during storage. It is very low in gluten. Garbanzos can also be roasted, covered in spices, and served as a savory snack.

Whole-wheat flour
Whole-wheat flour is a coarse-textured flour which is used to make bread, cakes, cookies, and pasta, as well as chapatis, parathas, and puris. Regular whole-wheat flour—which should be very well sifted before use —may also be used to make Indian breads. The flour is made by grinding the wheat kernel, which includes the bran, germ or embryo, and the endosperm. It has a high fiber content and is therefore healthier than white flour.

Brown Basmati rice
Apart from wheat, rice is the most widely cultivated cereal in the world. India is one of the largest consumers of rice worldwide. Basmati rice is an Indian rice, with very small, round grains and a distinctive flavor. Brown Basmati rice is wholegrain rice with only the outer husk removed, leaving the bran layers, and therefore has a characteristic grayish-tan color. It is more nutritious than white rice because, as only the outer husk has been removed, it retains some of the B vitamins, phosphorus, and starch. It is also high in fiber. It has a more nutty flavor and more chewy texture than white rice, and is becoming very popular in the West, largely because of the trend for a healthy, high-fiber diet. Always buy good quality Basmati rice, and soak it for 20–30 minutes before cooking, then drain well. Soaking prevents the rice sticking during the cooking process.

Sprouted mung beans
The mung bean is a bean plant, originating in the Far East. It is usually olive green in color, though it may also sometimes be yellow or

White Basmati rice

Gram flour

Masoor dhal

Dried moong dhal

black, and is spherical in shape. It should be thoroughly boiled for about 15 minutes to destroy any harmful toxins. The mung bean is widely cultivated for its shoots, which are popularly known as bean sprouts (or sprouted beans) and are delicious eaten either blanched or raw. Bean sprouts can be bought either fresh or canned from many stores specializing in Indian and Asian foods, as well as in many good food markets.

White Basmati rice
Basmati rice is a rice native to Asia, which has been grown for thousands of years and is widely associated with Indian cuisine. White Basmati rice is brown rice from which the germ and the outer layers have been removed by passing the grains through machines that rasp the grain. It has a more bland flavor than brown rice and is less nutritionally valuable, but it is nevertheless popular and widely used.

Masoor dhal
Masoor dhal is a small, round, dried red lentil, which has been husked and split. These split lentils should be cooked and added to dishes, or can be cooked with garlic, onion, and Indian spices as a dish in their own right. They are widely available in most food markets, and are labeled simply "lentils" or "red lentils." Lentils are nourishing and have a high energy content. They are particularly rich in protein, carbohydrates, phosphorus, and iron, as well as the B vitamins. Red lentils do not need to be soaked before cooking as they cook quickly without soaking.

Gram flour
This flour made from lentils or garbanzos, is used in India to thicken sauces, in curry powder and to make pakoras. It is finely milled to a light golden color and has a distinctive taste. Gram flour is also very useful for people who are allergic to gluten, a component of all wheat products. You can make your own substitute by finely grinding yellow split peas.

Moong dhal
Moong dhal is a dried whole or split yellow bean, which is tear drop shaped and has a green skin and yellow flesh. It also has a white stripe where the bean was attached to the pod. The beans are used in soups. They are more popular in northern India than in the south.

Chile Fry
with pepper and tomatoes

4 tablespoons vegetable oil

I large onion, finely chopped

½ teaspoon ground coriander seeds

½ teaspoon turmeric

I-inch piece of fresh ginger root, finely chopped

I chile, chopped

I pound steak, cut into strips about I x ½-inch thick

I green or red bell pepper, cored, seeded, and coarsely chopped

2 tomatoes, quartered

4 tablespoons lemon juice

salt

lemon wedges, to garnish

heat the oil in a skillet with a lid, add the onion, and cook until soft. Add the coriander, turmeric, ginger, and chile and cook over a low heat for 5 minutes; if the mixture becomes dry, add 1 tablespoon water.

add the strips of steak, increase the heat, and cook, stirring, until browned all over. Add the chopped bell pepper, cover, and simmer gently for 5–10 minutes, until the meat is tender. Add the tomatoes, lemon juice, and salt to taste and cook, uncovered, for 2–3 minutes. (This dish should be rather dry.) Serve, garnished with lemon wedges, if liked.

Serves 4
Preparation time: *5 minutes*
Cooking time: *35 minutes*

clipboard: Many Indian recipes require finely chopped ginger root. Here is a useful technique for doing this. Peel the piece of ginger root, and trim both ends flat. Stand on one end, and make a line of vertical cuts with a sharp knife. Holding the cut root together, turn it at right angles. Cut through again, making lines of fine strips. These can then be neatly chopped into small squares.

Aloo Cakes

Aloo is the Indian word for potato, which was not introduced to India until the 16th century.

3 tablespoons vegetable oil
I large onion, finely chopped
½-inch piece of fresh ginger root, finely chopped
I teaspoon ground coriander seeds
I cup ground beef
I tablespoon raisins
I tablespoon finely chopped fresh cilantro leaves
2 pounds potatoes, boiled and mashed with a little milk and salt
flour for coating
oil for shallow frying
salt
½ red bell pepper, sliced into strips
½ yellow bell pepper, sliced into strips
I-inch piece of mooli (winter radish) or a few radishes, very thinly sliced

heat the oil in a skillet, add the onion and ginger, and fry until golden. Add the ground coriander and ground beef and fry until brown.

add the raisins and salt to taste and simmer for about 20 minutes, until the meat is cooked. Spoon out any fat in the pan. Stir in the chopped cilantro and leave to cool.

divide the mashed potato into 8 portions. With well-floured hands, flatten each portion on one palm, put 3 teaspoons of the meat mixture in the center of each, and fold the potato over to cover. Form gently into a round patty shape.

dip the potato cakes lightly in flour and shallow fry, a few at a time, in hot oil, until crisp and golden, turning carefully to brown the underside.

serve with strips of red and yellow bell pepper and very thin slices of mooli or radish, if liked.

Serves 4
Preparation time: *1 hour*
Cooking time: *15 minutes*

Kofta in Yogurt

Spicy meatballs are fried until golden brown and crisp, and served with some plain yogurt and chopped cilantro.

2 cups ground beef
1½ cups fresh bread crumbs
2 fresh green chiles, finely chopped
1 onion, finely chopped
1-inch piece of fresh ginger root, finely chopped
2 teaspoons ground coriander seeds
1 egg, lightly beaten
oil for frying
2 cups plain yogurt
salt
2 tablespoons finely chopped fresh cilantro
leaves, to garnish

mix together the ground beef, bread crumbs, chiles, onion, ginger, ground coriander, salt to taste, and egg, and shape the mixture into walnut-sized balls.

heat the oil in a large pan, add the meatballs and fry until well browned and cooked through. Drain carefully.

pour the yogurt into a serving bowl and add the meatballs while still hot. Sprinkle with chopped cilantro and serve warm.

Serves 4
Preparation time: *15 minutes*
Cooking time: *15 minutes*

clipboard: Chop cilantro finely without cutting your fingers by using a mezzaluna, which you operate with a rocking motion until your herbs are chopped finely enough.

Balti Beef and Broccoli

with onion and chopped tomatoes

4 tablespoons ghee or vegetable oil

I large onion, chopped

2 garlic cloves, minced

I pound steak, cut into narrow strips

I tablespoon ground coriander

I teaspoon garam masala

I teaspoon chili powder

I teaspoon mustard powder

I x 8-oz can chopped tomatoes

8 ounces broccoli, washed and separated into flowerets, stalks sliced

salt

heat the ghee or oil in a heavy-bottom skillet and fry the onion until lightly browned. Add the garlic and cook for 1 minute further.

add the steak, increase the heat, and stir-fry until the steak is browned on all sides. Lower the heat, then cover and cook the meat in its own juices until tender, about 10 minutes.

stir in the coriander, garam masala, chili, mustard, and a pinch of salt, and stir-fry over a low heat for a few seconds. Stir in the canned chopped tomatoes and juice and cook, uncovered, until almost dry. Add the broccoli and stir-fry for a few minutes. Partly cover the skillet and simmer until tender, then serve at once.

Serves 4
Preparation time: *20 minutes*
Cooking time: *30 minutes*

clipboard: Chili powder varies according to its country of origin. Indian chili powder is made from the dried and ground flesh and seeds of red chiles and adds the hottest element to curry powder. It is very similar to cayenne pepper and the two can be used interchangeably.

Vegetarian

Fried Chile Cabbage
with potatoes, peas, and carrots

½ cup ghee or 2 tablespoons vegetable oil
I small onion, chopped
6 garlic cloves, minced
I teaspoon white cumin seeds
I teaspoon turmeric
I white cabbage, coarsely chopped
I cup diced potatoes
I cup shelled peas
I cup sliced carrots
8 ounces tomatoes, skinned and sliced
I teaspoon green mango powder
I fresh green chile, chopped
½ oz fresh ginger root, grated
I teaspoon garam masala
I tablespoon chopped fresh cilantro leaves
2 tablespoons melted butter, to serve

heat the ghee or vegetable oil in a large saucepan and fry the onion and garlic with the cumin seeds for about 5 minutes, until golden brown. Add the turmeric and shake the pan for a few seconds.

add the cabbage, potatoes, peas, and carrots. Cook, stirring continuously, for 5 minutes. Cover the pan and continue to cook gently over a low heat for a further 10 minutes.

stir in the tomatoes, green mango powder, chile, and ginger. Stir well and then replace the lid and continue cooking for 10 more minutes.

sprinkle the garam masala and chopped cilantro into the saucepan and stir well. Heat through over a low heat for about 5 minutes. Serve hot with the melted butter poured over the top.

Serves 4–6
Preparation time: *20 minutes*
Cooking time: *35 minutes*

clipboard: White cumin seeds have a similar, slightly sweetish aniseed flavor to fennel seeds.

Cauliflower Curry

½ cup ghee or 2 tablespoons vegetable oil
pinch of asafetida powder
1½ pounds cauliflower, cut into flowerets
1¼ cups plain yogurt
2 large onions, finely chopped
2 garlic cloves, minced
4 bay leaves
1¼ cups hot water
salt

Spices
6 cloves
6 black peppercorns
1 black cardamom
2 green cardamoms
2 x 1-inch pieces of cinnamon stick
1 teaspoon coriander seeds
1 teaspoon white cumin seeds
1 teaspoon red chili powder

heat one-quarter of the ghee or ½ teaspoon of vegetable oil in a large saucepan with the asafetida. Add the cauliflower and cook over a medium heat for 5 minutes. Using a slotted spoon, transfer the cauliflower to a bowl and pour the yogurt over the top.

add the remaining ghee or vegetable oil to the pan and when it is hot, add the onions, garlic, salt to taste, bay leaves, and all the spices except the chili powder. Fry until the onions are golden and soft and then stir in the chili powder.

return the cauliflower and yogurt to the pan and stir gently to combine all the ingredients. Cook gently over a low heat for 10 minutes.

pour in the hot water and simmer, stirring occasionally, for 25 minutes or until the cauliflower is tender. Serve this curry hot.

Serves 4–6
Preparation time: *15 minutes*
Cooking time: *45 minutes*

clipboard: Asafetida powder is formed from the sap that flows from the roots of a large plant which grows in India and looks a little like cow parsley. The roots are cut with a knife in early summer and the milky sap that seeps out of them turns into a hard, resin-like substance. This is then sold either in block form or ground into powder. Be careful to store it in an airtight container, as it has a strong and unpleasant smell. Luckily, this disappears on contact with heat, when a subtle oniony flavor develops. It is highly prized by members of certain Indian sects who are not allowed to eat onions. Use in small quantities.

Spinach with Tomatoes

Rich in both color and flavor, this delicious vegetable dish combines spinach with tomatoes, onions, and spices.

2 pounds fresh spinach

¾ cup ghee or 3 tablespoons vegetable oil

2 large onions, thinly sliced

2 garlic cloves, thinly sliced

5-oz piece of fresh ginger root, peeled and cut into strips ⅛ inch thick

2 teaspoons chili powder

2 teaspoons turmeric

2 teaspoons garam masala

2 teaspoons coriander seeds

1 teaspoon ground coriander

1 teaspoon cumin seeds

1½ teaspoons salt

2 teaspoons freshly ground black pepper

1 x 14-oz can tomatoes

wash the spinach thoroughly and then shake it dry. Remove any thick stalks and cut the spinach leaves into strips, about 1 inch wide.

heat the ghee or vegetable oil in a large, heavy-bottom saucepan and add the onions and garlic. Fry gently over a moderate heat for about 5 minutes until they are golden and soft.

add the ginger to the pan and cook gently for 5–6 minutes. Stir in the chili powder, turmeric, garam masala, coriander seeds, ground coriander, cumin seeds, salt and pepper and cook for 1 minute.

toss in the spinach and mix well to coat in the spice mixture. Add the tomatoes with their juice and bring to the boil, stirring. Add enough boiling water to prevent the spinach sticking to the bottom of the pan. Simmer for 5–10 minutes, until the spinach and tomatoes are cooked.

Serves 4–6
Preparation time: *15 minutes*
Cooking time: *20–25 minutes*

Stuffed Eggplants

4–6 eggplants, halved lengthwise

½ cup water

1 bay leaf

½ cup ghee or 2 tablespoons vegetable oil

1 large onion, finely chopped

2 garlic cloves, finely chopped

2 teaspoons coriander seeds

1 teaspoon chili powder

1 teaspoon lovage seeds (optional)

1 teaspoon salt

To garnish

fresh cilantro leaves

dried red chiles, chopped

place the eggplants in a roasting pan with the cut sides upward. Pour in the water, add the bay leaf, and cover the pan tightly with foil. Cook in a preheated oven at 325°F for 25 minutes, or until soft.

heat the ghee or vegetable oil in a heavy-bottom saucepan and gently fry the onion and garlic for 4–5 minutes, until soft. Crush the coriander seeds coarsely and add to the onion mixture with the chili powder, lovage seeds, if using, and salt. Stir well and fry for 2–3 minutes.

remove the poached eggplants from the water and pat dry with paper towels. With a teaspoon, scrape out the flesh, reserving the skins. Mash the eggplant flesh and add to the spice mixture. Fry for 2–3 minutes, stirring.

grill or broil the eggplant skins for 5 minutes until dried out, and fill with the fried mixture. Arrange on a serving dish and serve garnished with cilantro leaves and chiles.

Serves 4–6
Preparation time: *20 minutes*
Cooking time: *35 minutes*
Oven temperature: 325°F

clipboard: Lovage is an aromatic herb, originally from Persia. The leaves taste rather like celery, and the seeds can also be used and go particularly well with vegetables. The leaf stalks can be candied, rather like angelica.

Cream Cheese Kofta Curry

2 pounds potatoes, quartered

I large fresh green chile, chopped

I teaspoon peeled and grated fresh ginger root

½ teaspoon garam masala

2 tablespoons garbanzo or gram flour

2 tablespoons fresh bread crumbs

I tablespoon roasted coriander seeds, ground

8 ounces panir

I tablespoon shredded or desiccated coconut

I egg white, beaten

¾ cup ghee or 3 tablespoons vegetable oil

2 bay leaves

2 onions, chopped

6 garlic cloves, minced

4 cloves

6 black peppercorns

⅝ cup plain yogurt

I teaspoon turmeric

I teaspoon chili powder

I¼ cups water

I pound tomatoes, skinned and sliced

2 tablespoons chopped fresh cilantro leaves

salt

boil the potatoes in some water with the green chile, ginger, and all but a pinch of the garam masala. When tender, drain the potatoes and mash with a little salt, the garbanzo or gram flour, bread crumbs and coriander. Divide into 12 equal-sized portions.

mix the panir with the coconut and the remaining garam masala. Divide into 12 equal-sized portions. Flatten the potato portions and use to wrap around the panir portions. Roll into balls, brush with beaten egg white, and fry in a skillet in the heated ghee or oil until golden brown. Drain and transfer to an ovenproof dish.

add the bay leaves, onions, garlic, cloves, and peppercorns to the ghee or oil left in the skillet and fry until golden. Stir in the yogurt, turmeric, and chili powder. Add the water and bring to the boil. Reduce the heat and simmer for 10 minutes.

pour this sauce over the koftas and cover with the tomatoes and cilantro leaves. Cook in a preheated oven at 350°F for 10–15 minutes, or until heated through. Serve immediately.

Serves 4–6
Preparation time: *30 minutes*
Cooking time: *1 hour*
Oven temperature: 350°F

clipboard: To skin a tomato, put it in a bowl, pour boiling water on to it, and leave for 2–3 minutes. Remove the tomato, pierce the skin with the point of a knife, and the skin will then come away easily.

Vegetable Rolls
with quick chutney

5 potatoes, boiled and coarsely mashed

2 tablespoons chopped fresh cilantro leaves

2 fresh green chiles, seeded and chopped

2 teaspoons lime juice

I teaspoon garam masala

oil for deep frying

salt and freshly ground black pepper

Quick chutney

I large bunch of fresh cilantro leaves

3 fresh green chiles, seeded and chopped

I teaspoon sugar

½ teaspoon salt

3 tablespoons grated fresh coconut

juice of ½ lime

Batters

½ cup garbanzo bean or gram flour (besan)

I½ cups all-purpose flour

I¼ cups water

pinch of chili powder

I teaspoon baking powder

I¼ cups milk

ghee or vegetable oil for frying

salt

To serve

I small onion, chopped

I carrot, grated

¼ crisp lettuce, shredded

start by making the quick chutney: trim the stalks from the cilantro and grind the leaves with the chiles, sugar, salt, coconut, and lime juice to make a paste. You can do this either by pounding in a mortar or by grinding in a blender or food processor. Put to one side.

prepare the filling for the pancake rolls: mix together the potatoes, cilantro, chiles, lime juice, garam masala, salt and pepper. Shape the potato mixture into rolls, about 1 inch in diameter and 4 inches in length. Set aside.

make the two batters: mix the garbanzo bean or gram flour with one-third of the all-purpose flour and beat in the water to make a batter for the potato rolls. Add the salt and chili powder and set aside. Mix the remaining all-purpose flour with the baking powder and a pinch of salt. Beat in the milk to make a smooth batter.

heat a little ghee or vegetable oil in a small skillet and pour in some batter, swirling it around the skillet to form a thick pancake. Cook until browned underneath, flip over, and cook the other side. Repeat with the remaining batter. Layer the pancakes with paper towels and keep warm.

heat the oil for deep frying to 350°F. Dip the potato rolls in the prepared water batter and then deep fry, a few at a time, until golden. Remove and drain. Spread each pancake with a little of the prepared chutney and then top with a potato roll and some onion, carrot, and lettuce. Fold over and serve.

Serves 6
Preparation time: *40 minutes*
Cooking time: *10–15 minutes*

Spicy Okra

This mild curry made with fresh okra, or "ladies' fingers," and tomatoes is both flavored and garnished with fresh mint.

2 large onions, peeled
½ cup ghee or 2 tablespoons vegetable oil
4 garlic cloves
2 teaspoons ground coriander
½ teaspoon turmeric
I pound fresh okra, trimmed and cut into ½-inch slices
2 tomatoes, skinned and chopped
I teaspoon chopped fresh mint
½ teaspoon garam masala
salt and freshly ground black pepper
fresh mint, to garnish

slice one of the onions very thinly. Heat the ghee or vegetable oil in a heavy-bottom saucepan and add the sliced onion. Fry gently until tender and golden brown.

chop the remaining onion and place in a blender or food processor with the garlic, seasoning, coriander, and turmeric. Process until the mixture is well blended.

stir the blended onion and spice mixture into the fried onion in the saucepan and cook over a medium heat for 5 minutes, stirring occasionally.

add the okra to the pan. Stir gently and then simmer, covered, for 20 minutes. Add the tomatoes, chopped mint, and garam masala and simmer for 15 minutes. Serve garnished with fresh mint.

Serves 4
Preparation time: *10 minutes*
Cooking time: *45 minutes*

clipboard: Okra is a tropical plant grown for its pods, which have longitudinal ridges and under-ripe seeds inside them. Okra can be bought from most large food markets all year round and is also available dried and in cans. It is particularly rich in calcium, phosphorus, iron, and vitamin C.

Phul Gobi
with multicolored bell peppers

3 tablespoons oil

I onion, sliced

½ teaspoon turmeric

I cauliflower, broken into flowerets

2 fresh green chiles, seeded

I green bell pepper, cored, seeded, and cut into strips

I yellow bell pepper, cored, seeded, and cut into strips

I red bell pepper, cored, seeded, and cut into strips

salt

heat the oil in a pan, add the onion, and fry until soft. Add the turmeric and cook for 1 minute. Add the cauliflower flowerets and salt to taste. Stir well, cover the pan, and cook gently for about 10 minutes, until the cauliflower is almost cooked.

add the chiles and bell peppers, stir, and cook for a further 5 minutes, or until tender.

Serves 4
Preparation time: *5 minutes*
Cooking time: *25–30 minutes*

clipboard: The combination of green, yellow, and red bell peppers in this recipe makes it a really attractive dish. The preparation time is a lot shorter than the cooking time, making it a quick and easy recipe to add to your repertoire.

Vegetables, herbs and fruit

Bay leaves

Mango

Coconut

Ginger

Cayenne peppers

Bird's eye chile peppers

Bay leaves
Bay is not a true herb but the leaf of the laurel tree. Because of its strong aroma, however, it is often treated as a herb. Traditionally, bay leaves were used in Roman times to crown victors in cultural or sporting events. Bay requires long slow cooking in order for the full flavor to develop.

Mango
The mango is a sweet tropical fruit, whose golden flesh is surrounded by smooth, red, yellow, or green skin. It has a large single seed and can be eaten by itself or used in curries, chutneys, or ice cream. Mangoes are at their best in summer but are available canned all year round.

Cayenne peppers
Perhaps the best-known chile pepper, although usually bought as cayenne pepper, which is made by crushing the dried pods.

Coconut
The coconut is a large nut, the fruit of the coconut palm, which grows in the tropics. The flesh of the coconut is white and rich in oil, and the nut also contains a translucent liquid. The soft pulp can be eaten by itself or incorporated in different forms in both sweet and savory dishes. The liquid also makes a refreshing drink, which can be drunk by itself or mixed with alcohol.

Bird's eye chile peppers
Also known as Mexican Peanuts, these tiny bead-like peppers measure just ¼ inch across. Their small size belies their fiery taste, so they should only be used sparingly.

Ginger
Ginger is a brown, knobbly root, which has a pale golden flesh. It is used to flavor both sweet and savory dishes and is used extensively in Indian cooking. The root must be peeled and finely chopped before being added to dishes. Ground ginger is often used in desserts. Ginger can also be pickled, preserved, or crystallized.

Eggplant
The eggplant derives its name from its distinctive shape. It is, in fact, a fruit but is usually cooked and eaten as a vegetable. It has dark, smooth purple skin

Cilantro

Curry leaves

Eggplant

Garlic

Jalapeño chiles

Okra

Mint

and pale greenish cream flesh. It can be steamed, boiled, broiled, or sautéed.

Mint
Mint is a very fragrant herb with a strong fresh flavor. There are 25 different varieties of mint, all of which have bright green leaves and small white flowers. It is used extensively in many Indian dishes, especially with lamb. Fresh mint is a good garnish. It can also be dried.

Curry leaves
The small glossy evergreen curry leaves look similar to those of the bay tree. They should be used fresh or, if they are dried, as an ingredient in curry powder. Curry leaves may be chopped, crumbled, fried, or powdered.

Garlic
Garlic is a bulb-shaped root vegetable. The bulb is arranged as a series of cloves which are wrapped in a papery white skin. Garlic has been in popular use for centuries, and has been a powerful ingredient in the history of cooking. It is also prized for its health-giving properties, being used to treat various ailments and ward off evil spirits. The pungent aroma and flavour of garlic adds character to any dish.

Cilantro (coriander)
Cilantro is a member of the carrot family. It has bright green, lacy leaves, which have a strong aroma and flavor, and little white flowers. The leaves, roots, and seeds are all used in cooking and are used extensively in many Indian dishes. The leaves make an attractive garnish.

Jalapeño chiles
A well-known, versatile chile which can be either green or red. It is a fleshy, almost sausage-shaped fruit, 2½–3 inches long and has a very hot taste.

Okra
Okra, also known as "ladies' fingers," is a finger-sized green pod, pointed at one end, which contains small white seeds. It can be cooked whole or sliced and is popular in Indian cookery. It is gelatinous when cooked and can be used as a thickening agent. It is in season from summer through to fall.

Panir Mattar

A combination of peas with curd cheese, this is a favorite vegetable dish in many Indian restaurants. Follow this recipe and you won't even need to go out to enjoy it.

2–3 tablespoons oil

4 ounces panir (curd cheese), cut into ½-inch cubes

2 tablespoons finely chopped onion

5 tablespoons water

2 cups shelled peas

½ teaspoon sugar

1 tablespoon grated fresh ginger root

2 fresh green chiles, finely chopped

½ teaspoon garam masala

1 tablespoon finely chopped fresh cilantro

salt

heat the oil in a heavy-bottom pan, add the panir, and fry until golden, turning gently and taking care not to burn it. Remove from the pan and set aside. Add the onions to the pan and fry until colored; remove, and set aside.

add the water, and salt to taste, to the pan and bring to the boil. Add the peas and sugar, cover, and simmer until the peas are almost tender. If necessary, uncover and cook for 1 minute to evaporate any liquid.

return the onions to the pan, add the ginger and chiles, and stir well. Cook for 2 minutes, then very gently stir in the panir. Heat through for 2 minutes, then stir in the garam masala and cilantro. Serve immediately.

Serves 4
Preparation time: *5 minutes*
Cooking time: *25 minutes*

clipboard: Panir is an Indian curd cheese used in cooking. It is available from some gourmet and Indian specialist food stores. It goes particularly well with vegetable dishes made with peas or spinach.

Gram and Bean Dhal *with squash and chile*

5 cups water

⅔ cup split grams or yellow split peas

⅔ cup dried beans

½ teaspoon turmeric

4 ounces peeled and sliced squash, cut into
2-inch pieces

½ cup ghee or 2 tablespoons vegetable oil

I onion, finely chopped

6 garlic cloves, minced

I teaspoon white cumin seeds

I fresh green chile, chopped

I dried red chile, crushed

½ teaspoon chili powder

salt

fried onions, to garnish

bring the water to the boil in a large saucepan. Meanwhile, wash the grams or split peas and beans in a colander under cold running water and then drain well.

tip the drained grams and beans into the boiling water with a good pinch of salt and the turmeric. Bring the water back to the boil, cover the pan, and simmer for 1½ hours, stirring occasionally.

add the marrow to the pan with the grams and beans. Simmer gently for a further 30 minutes.

heat the ghee or vegetable oil in a skillet and fry the onion, garlic, and cumin until golden brown. Remove from the heat and add the chiles and chili powder.

serve the dhal hot with the fried onion sprinkled on top.

Serves 6
Preparation time: *15 minutes*
Cooking time: *2 hours*

Sprouting Mung Dhal

with fennel seeds and ginger

8 ounces whole mung beans, rinsed

3–4 tablespoons oil

1 onion, thinly sliced

2 fresh green chiles, seeded and chopped

1 inch piece of fresh ginger root, cut into fine matchsticks

1 teaspoon fennel seeds

1¼ cups water

salt

place the beans in a bowl a day before they are required, and barely cover them with warm water. Cover the bowl with plastic wrap and leave in a warm dark place. Do not let the beans dry out; add a little extra water if necessary. The beans will have sprouted by the next day. Rinse and drain them.

heat the oil in a saucepan. Add the onion and fry, stirring, for 3 minutes. Stir in the chiles, ginger, and fennel seeds and cook, stirring, until the onions have softened a little.

add the beans, salt to taste, and the water. Bring to simmering point, cover, and cook gently, stirring occasionally, for 25–30 minutes, or until the beans are soft and there is no liquid left.

Serves 4
Preparation time: *15 minutes*, plus
   overnight standing time
Cooking time: *30 minutes*

clipboard: Mung beans come from a bean plant, called haricot mungo, originating from the Far East, with small green yellow or brown seeds.

Aloo Sag

Potatoes and spinach are happy partners, whose flavors complement each other wonderfully in this delicious vegetarian dish.

6 tablespoons oil

1 onion, chopped

1 inch piece of fresh ginger root, chopped

2 fresh green chiles, finely chopped

1 teaspoon turmeric

2 garlic cloves, finely chopped

1 pound potatoes, cut into small pieces

2 x 8-oz packets frozen spinach leaf, thawed

salt

heat the oil in a lidded skillet, add the onion, and cook until soft. Add the ginger, chiles, turmeric, and garlic and cook for 5 minutes. Add the potatoes, and salt to taste, stir well, cover, and cook for 10 minutes.

squeeze out any liquid from the spinach and chop. Add to the potatoes and cook for about 5 minutes, until both vegetables are tender.

Serves 4
Preparation time: *5 minutes*
Cooking time: *30 minutes*

clipboard: This recipe uses frozen spinach leaf, thawed, but you could equally well use fresh if you prefer, which would give both a slightly stronger colour and flavour.

Tamatar Aloo

An interesting way of cooking potatoes and tomatoes with spices and lemon juice, this is a fantastic vegetarian dish. Serve it either with other vegetables, or to accompany a meat dish.

2 tablespoons oil
½ teaspoon mustard seeds
8 ounces potatoes, cut into small cubes
1 teaspoon turmeric
1 teaspoon chili powder
2 teaspoons paprika
4 tablespoons lemon juice
1 teaspoon sugar
8 ounces tomatoes, quartered
salt
2 tablespoons finely chopped cilantro leaves, to garnish

heat the oil in a saucepan, add the mustard seeds, and cook until they pop—this should only take a few seconds. Add the potatoes and fry for about 5 minutes. Add the spices, lemon juice, sugar, and salt to taste, stir well, and cook for 5 minutes.

add the tomatoes, stir well, then simmer for 5–10 minutes, until the potatoes are tender. Serve garnished with cilantro leaves.

Serves 4
Preparation time: *5 minutes*
Cooking time: *20 minutes*

clipboard: Turmeric is often regarded as a poor man's saffron—largely because it so much less expensive. It has a more bitter taste than saffron and is an ingredient in commercial curry powders. Be careful not to spill it as it stains clothing and work surfaces.

Bharta

This is definitely one of the most interesting dishes you can produce with eggplants—simple, quick, slightly spicy, and utterly delicious.

1 pound eggplants
2 tablespoons oil
1 large onion, finely chopped
1 garlic clove, minced
1 fresh green chile, seeded and chopped
1 tablespoon ground coriander seeds
1 tablespoon finely chopped fresh cilantro leaves, plus extra to garnish
1 tablespoon lemon juice
salt

cook the eggplants in a preheated oven at 350°F for 30 minutes, or until they are soft.

cool slightly, then slit open, scoop out all the eggplant flesh, and mash it with a fork.

heat the oil in a pan, add the onion, garlic, and chile, and fry until the onion is soft but not colored.

add the ground coriander, fresh cilantro, and salt to taste. Add the mashed eggplant, stir well, and cook, uncovered, for 2 minutes, then cover and simmer very gently for 5 minutes. Sprinkle with lemon juice and serve, garnished with cilantro leaves.

Serves 4
Preparation time: *40 minutes*
Cooking time: *20 minutes*
Oven temperature: 350°F

clipboard: Coriander is used extensively in Indian cooking, both as a spice and as a herb (cilantro). The seeds have a warm fruity flavor and have been used for hundreds of years, while the cilantro leaves have only regained their popularity in recent years. Coriander seeds are equally good used either on their own or combined with other spices. They are one of the ingredients in commercial curry powder.

Kabli Channa

The only difficult thing about this recipe is remembering to soak the grams overnight. The rest is easy!

1⅓ cups whole Bengal grams (or split red lentils)

3 cups water

1 teaspoon salt

2 tablespoons ghee or vegetable oil

1 onion, chopped

1-inch piece of cinnamon stick

4 cloves

2 garlic cloves, minced

1-inch piece of fresh ginger root, chopped

2 fresh green chiles, finely chopped

2 teaspoons ground coriander seeds

½ cup chopped tomatoes

1 teaspoon garam masala

1 tablespoon finely chopped fresh cilantro leaves, to garnish

wash the grams (or lentils) and soak in the water overnight. Add the salt and simmer until tender. Drain, reserving the water, and set aside.

heat the ghee or oil in a pan, add the onion, and cook until golden. Add the cinnamon and cloves and fry for a few seconds, then add the garlic, ginger, chiles, and ground coriander and fry for 5 minutes. Add the tomatoes and cook until most of the liquid has evaporated.

add the grams (or lentils) and cook gently for 5 minutes, then add the reserved water and simmer for 20–25 minutes. Add the garam masala and stir well. Sprinkle with the chopped cilantro and serve immediately.

Serves 4
Preparation time: *30 minutes*, plus overnight soaking time
Cooking time: *45–50 minutes*

clipboard: Grams are garbanzo beans or lentils. When ground, they are used to make gram flour, a common ingredient in Indian cookery.

Vegetable Curry

No Indian meal is complete without a vegetable curry. This one combines eggplants, peas, potatoes, and tomatoes, lightly spiced with fennel seeds, chili powder, coriander seeds, and fresh green chiles. Simply delicious!

3 tablespoons oil

1 teaspoon fennel seeds

2 onions, sliced

1 teaspoon chili powder

1 tablespoon ground coriander seeds

1-inch piece of fresh ginger root, chopped

2 eggplants, sliced

1½ cups shelled peas

4 ounces potatoes, cubed

1 x 8-oz can chopped tomatoes

4 green chiles, sliced

salt

heat the oil in a large pan, add the fennel seeds, and fry for a few seconds. Add the onions and fry until soft and golden. Add the chili powder, coriander, ginger, and salt to taste. Cook for 2 minutes, stirring. Add the eggplants, peas, and potatoes and cook for 5 minutes, stirring occasionally.

add the tomatoes, along with their juice, and the chiles to the pan, cover and simmer for 30 minutes, or until the peas and potatoes are tender and the sauce is thick.

Serves 4
Preparation time: *20 minutes*
Cooking time: *30 minutes*

Balti Mixed Vegetables

Use whichever vegetables are in season, finely diced so that they do not take too long to become tender. The flavors are a subtle blend of ginger, chili, coriander, and turmeric.

2–3 tablespoons vegetable oil
1 small onion, chopped
1 garlic clove, minced
1-inch piece of fresh ginger root, grated
1 teaspoon chili powder
2 teaspoons ground coriander
½ teaspoon ground turmeric
1 pound diced mixed vegetables (e.g. potatoes, carrots, swede, peas, beans, cauliflower)
2–3 tomatoes, skinned and chopped, or
4 tablespoons lemon juice
salt

heat the oil in a large wok or heavy-bottom saucepan and gently fry the onion for 5–10 minutes, or until lightly browned. Add the garlic, ginger, chili powder, coriander, turmeric, and a pinch of salt. Fry for 2–3 minutes, add the diced vegetables, and stir-fry for a further 2–3 minutes.

add either the chopped tomatoes or the lemon juice. Stir well and add a little water.

cover and cook gently for 10–12 minutes, or until the vegetables are tender, adding a little more water, if necessary, to prevent the vegetables sticking to the bottom of the wok or pan.

serve at once with chapatis or naan (see pages 200 and 202).

Serves 4
Preparation time: *15 minutes*
Cooking time: *20–30 minutes*

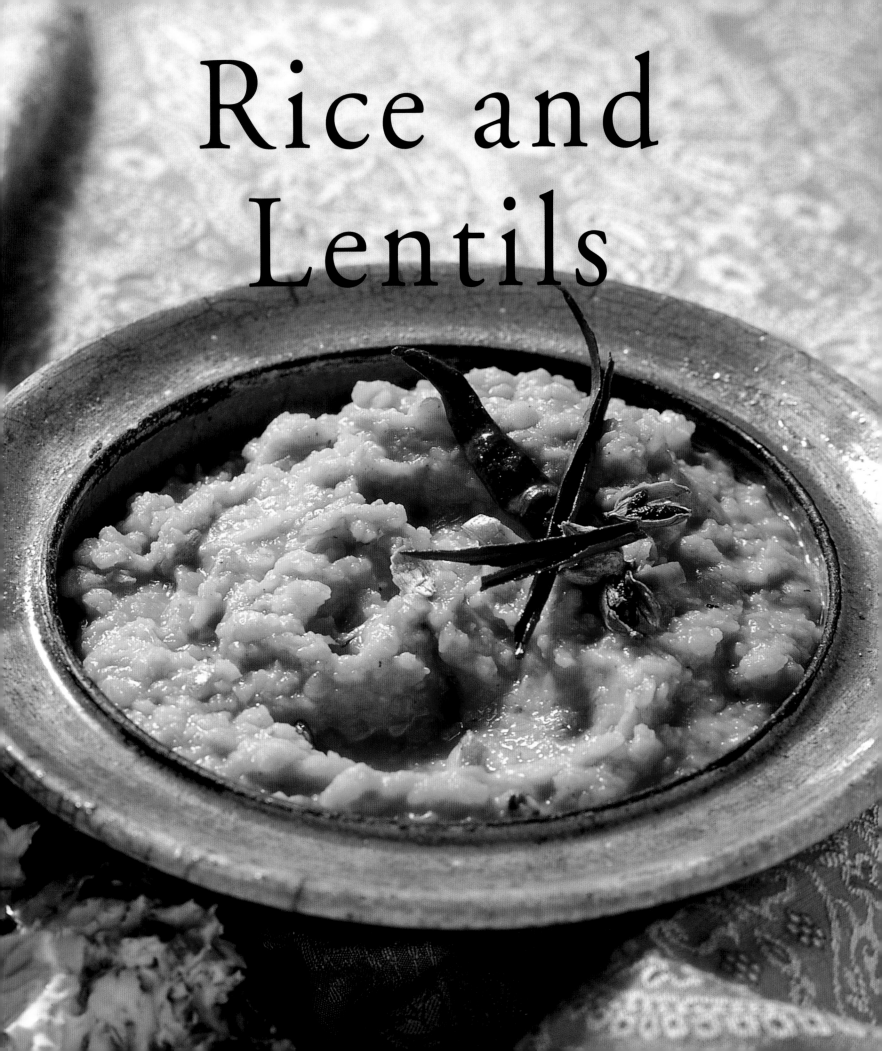

Rice and Lentils

Saffron Rice

The combination of rice with saffron threads was made in heaven! This is not the simplest way of cooking rice, but is well worth the effort.

½ teaspoon saffron threads
3 cups boiling water
¾ cup ghee or 3 tablespoons vegetable oil
2 large onions, sliced
1½ cups Basmati or Patna rice
1 teaspoon cloves
4 cardamoms
1 teaspoon salt
1 teaspoon freshly ground black pepper
silver leaf (varq), to garnish (optional)

put the saffron threads in a small bowl with 1 tablespoon boiling water and leave to soak for 30 minutes. Heat the ghee or vegetable oil in a large heavy-bottom saucepan, then add the onions. Cook gently for 4–5 minutes until soft.

wash the Basmati or Patna rice thoroughly in a strainer under cold running water and drain well.

add the rice to the onions in the pan and then stir in the cloves, cardamoms, salt and pepper. Fry for 3 minutes, stirring frequently.

pour the remaining boiling water into the pan, together with the saffron and its soaking liquid, then lower the heat and simmer for 15–20 minutes, until the rice is cooked.

drain well and transfer the rice to a serving dish. Serve hot, garnished, if liked, with silver leaf.

Serves 4
Preparation time: *15 minutes*, plus
30 minutes soaking time
Cooking time: *30–35 minutes*

clipboard: Varq is edible silver leaf, used for decorative purposes. It is very fragile and should therefore be handled with care. It is available from specialist Indian food stores, though you may have to order it.

Rice with Vegetables

8 ounces frozen diced mixed vegetables

4 ounces frozen diced red and green bell peppers

4 ounces zucchini, trimmed and sliced

2 tablespoons ground cumin

2 tablespoons ground coriander

1 tablespoon chili powder

2 teaspoons turmeric

4 teaspoons black peppercorns, crushed

2 teaspoons salt

½ cup ghee or 2 tablespoons vegetable oil

4 large onions, thinly sliced

5 garlic cloves, thinly sliced

2 x 3-inch pieces of fresh ginger root, peeled and sliced

2 x 3-inch pieces of cinnamon stick

20 cardamoms

20 cloves

1 tablespoon lovage seeds (optional)

3 cups Basmati rice, washed and drained

8¾ cups boiling water

½ cup golden raisins, to serve

½ cup slivered almonds, to serve

mix the frozen vegetables with the zucchini and set aside to defrost. Mix together the ground spices and salt. Heat half of the ghee or vegetable oil in a large saucepan, add half of the spice mixture, and fry gently for 2 minutes. Stir in the vegetables to coat with the spices and then remove and keep warm.

heat the remaining ghee or vegetable oil in the saucepan and add the onions, garlic, and ginger. Fry gently for 5 minutes, until soft. Add the pieces of cinnamon stick, cardamoms, cloves, and lovage seeds, if using, and fry for 3–4 minutes. Add the remaining spice mixture and fry for 2 minutes.

add the Basmati rice to the saucepan and stir well until all the grains are coated with the spices. Pour in the boiling water and boil gently, uncovered, until the rice is cooked but still firm. Stir occasionally to prevent the rice sticking, adding more boiling water, if necessary.

drain the rice, when ready, into a large sieve. Mix with the reserved vegetables and serve scattered with golden raisins and almonds.

Serves 6–8
Preparation time: *15 minutes*
Cooking time: *35–40 minutes*

Spices

Saffron

Coriander seeds

Cardamom pods

Dried red chiles

Cardamom pods

The cardamom pod is a small, pale green, oval-shaped pod, which protects some small black seeds. Cardamom is a member of the ginger family. It is a highly aromatic spice and is essential to Indian cuisine. The pods are picked before they are ripe and, when they are dried, they can be ground or used whole. Cardamom is one of the main ingredients in curry powder. It is also used in pickles and rice dishes, and is very good in certain sweet dishes. It should be used sparingly as it is an expensive spice, as each pod has to be hand picked. Cardamom seeds are often chewed after a meal as a breath freshener.

Saffron threads

These are made from the dried, thread-like stamens of the saffron crocus. The stamens are a dark orange color and are highly fragrant. Saffron is the most expensive and most highly prized spice on the market, as each crocus has three stamens and each one must be hand picked. Saffron threads are used in fish dishes, rice, and many other Asian and Indian dishes. They are also used in some sweet recipes, such as ice cream and cookies. In order to use saffron, the strands can be either soaked in hot milk, water, or stock for 15 minutes before being added to a dish, or they can be roasted in a metal spoon directly over a low heat until they are crisp enough to be crushed.

Coriander seeds

The small oval coriander seeds have a particularly fine lemony flavor. They can be used whole, ground, or roasted. Coriander seeds are a very important ingredient in curry powder, and they can also be used in pickles, chutney, and marinades.

Dried red chiles

Tiny red peppers with a fiercely fiery heat, chiles were first grown in the Amazon region of South America and in Mexico. Their arrival in India, where they were exported to the trading posts, was to revolutionize Indian cooking. Dried chiles are easy to use: simply cut off the stalks, shake out the seeds, and then break the chile into little pieces and cover these with hot water.

Cinnamon

Cumin seeds

Chilli powder

Turmeric

Leave for 15–20 minutes and then drain, reserving the water. Chop the chiles coarsely and put them in a small blender or electric mill with half the soaking water and process to a purée. Chiles must be used with caution, as they are profoundly hot and can even damage the mucus membrane inside the mouth, nose, throat, stomach, and intestine if used in too large quantities. The best remedy for a burning sensation after eating chiles is cold dairy food such as yogurt, milk, or ice cream. If they are stored properly, chiles will keep for ever and maintain both their attractive red color and their fiery taste.

Turmeric
This is a spice taken from the dried roots of a tropical plant related to the ginger family. Turmeric is ground to produce a bright yellow powder. It has a mild bittersweet flavor and is used in pickles, chutneys, and mustard. In Thailand, the roots are boiled and used as a vegetable, but in Indian cuisine it is mainly used as a coloring agent to impart a strong yellow to foods, particularly rice dishes.

Cinnamon
Cinnamon is a popular bark-like spice, which is light brown in color and has a strong, sweet aroma. It comes from an evergreen tree in Sri Lanka, and is often used in soups, baking, liqueurs, and oils.

Chili powder
This is the combination of ground, dried chile peppers and other seasonings. It is a dark red powder with a spicy, peppery taste. It is used to flavor many chile dishes, one of the most popular being Chile Con Carne. It should be used sparingly because of its strong flavor. When buying chili powder, purchase small amounts as it has a limited shelf life and rapidly loses its flavor.

Cumin seeds
The seeds of the cumin plant are long and pale brown. They are very aromatic with a pungent flavor. Cumin seeds are one of the most important spices in Indian cuisine, and are used in most dishes. The seeds can be roasted to bring out their flavor.

Kitcheree

Basmati rice is cooked with yellow lentils and gently spiced with cloves, cardamom seeds, a piece of cinnamon stick, and turmeric.

1 cup Basmati rice
1⅓ cups yellow lentils (moong dhal)
5 tablespoons ghee or 1½ tablespoons vegetable oil
1 garlic clove, sliced
5 cloves
5 cardamom seeds
2-inch piece of cinnamon stick
1 small onion, sliced
1 teaspoon turmeric
½ teaspoon salt

To garnish
fried onion rings
chopped fresh cilantro leaves

mix the rice and lentils together and then wash thoroughly in cold running water. Drain well, place in a bowl, and cover with cold water. Leave to soak for 1 hour.

heat the ghee or vegetable oil in a large pan and fry the garlic, cloves, cardamom seeds, and cinnamon for 1 minute. Add the onion and cook for 1–2 minutes.

drain the rice and lentils thoroughly and then add them to the onion and spices in the pan. Stir in the turmeric and salt, and toss gently over a low heat for 5 minutes.

add enough boiling water to cover the rice by 1 inch, and then cover the pan with a tightly fitting lid. Simmer over a low heat for 30–45 minutes, until the rice is cooked and the liquid absorbed. Serve garnished with fried onion rings and chopped cilantro.

Serves 4
Preparation time: *15 minutes*, plus
  1 hour soaking time
Cooking time: *40–55 minutes*

Vegetable Biriyani

Vegetables and rice are cooked together to make a glorious one-pot meal. A mixture of curd cheese, golden raisins, and nuts, including almonds, cashews, and pistachios, is the perfect finishing touch.

3 tablespoons ghee or vegetable oil

1 large onion, finely chopped

2 garlic cloves, chopped

8 cloves

2 x 1-inch pieces of cinnamon stick

4 green cardamoms

1 teaspoon turmeric

1 teaspoon garam masala

2 cups Basmati rice, pre-soaked

8 ounces mixed diced vegetables (e.g. carrots, cauliflower, zucchini, okra, peas)

2½ cups Vegetable Stock (see page 11)

2 ounces panir (curd cheese), lightly fried

⅓ cup golden raisins

1 cup chopped mixed nuts (e.g. almonds, cashews, pistachios)

salt

heat the ghee or vegetable oil in a large saucepan and fry the onion until golden. Remove half of the fried onion and set aside for the garnish. Add the garlic and spices to the pan and fry for 2–3 minutes.

rinse the Basmati rice in cold running water and then drain well. Add to the pan and stir well. Cook for a further 5 minutes, until all the grains are glistening and translucent.

add the mixed diced vegetables and salt to taste, together with the stock, and bring to the boil. Cover the pan and reduce the heat to a bare simmer. Cook gently for 20–25 minutes, until all the liquid has been absorbed and the rice is cooked.

stir in the panir, golden raisins and nuts and mix well. Cover and cook for 5 minutes over a low heat until all the moisture has evaporated. Serve hot, sprinkled with the reserved fried onion.

Serves 4–6
Preparation time: *15 minutes*
Cooking time: *40–45 minutes*

Masoor Dhal

This spicy lentil dish, flavored with onion, garlic, and lemon juice, is high in nutrients as well as tasting delicious, so you can feel good about its benefits as well as enjoying its fantastic flavors.

4 tablespoons oil
6 cloves
6 cardamoms
1-inch piece of cinnamon stick
1 onion, chopped
1-inch piece of fresh ginger root, chopped
1 fresh green chile, finely chopped
1 garlic clove, chopped
½ teaspoon garam masala
1⅓ cups lentils
4 tablespoons lemon juice
salt
2–3 dried chiles, to garnish (optional)

heat the oil in a pan, add the cloves, cardamoms, and cinnamon and fry until they start to swell.

add the onion and cook until translucent. Add the ginger, chile, garlic, and garam masala and cook for about 5 minutes.

add the lentils, stir thoroughly, and cook for 1 minute. Add salt to taste and enough water to come about 1¼ inches above the level of the lentils. Bring to the boil, cover, and simmer for about 20 minutes, until really thick and tender.

sprinkle with the lemon juice, stir and serve immediately, garnished with dried chiles, if liked.

Serves 4
Preparation time: *20 minutes*
Cooking time: *25 minutes*

clipboard: Lentils are full of nutrients and have a high energy value. They are rich in protein, carbohydrates, phosphorus, and iron, as well as the B vitamins.

Shrimp and Spinach Rice

2 cups Basmati rice

2 teaspoons salt

½ teaspoon turmeric

4 tablespoons butter

3 tablespoons oil

2 onions sliced

3 garlic cloves, finely chopped

I tablespoon grated fresh ginger root

I–2 teaspoons chili powder

2 teaspoons ground coriander

2 pounds spinach, washed, trimmed, and chopped

I pound cooked peeled shrimp

place the Basmati rice in a strainer and wash it thoroughly under cold running water. Drain well. Fill a large saucepan two-thirds full with water and bring to the boil. Add the rice to the saucepan together with 1 teaspoon of the salt and the turmeric. Boil for 3 minutes and then drain. Stir in the butter.

heat the oil in a large saucepan and add the onions, garlic, and ginger. Fry for 5 minutes until golden. Stir in the chili powder, coriander, and the remaining 1 teaspoon of salt, and fry for a few seconds.

add the spinach and cook, stirring constantly, until softened. Stir in the shrimp and then remove from the heat.

layer the spinach mixture with the buttered rice in an ovenproof casserole dish, beginning and ending with the spinach. Cover tightly with a lid and then cook in a preheated oven at 350°F for 30 minutes. Serve immediately.

Serves 4
Preparation time: *30 minutes*
Cooking time: *30 minutes*
Oven temperature: 350°F

Pilau Rice
with mixed nuts

2 tablespoons ghee or vegetable oil
6 cardamoms, bruised
5 whole cloves
3-inch piece of cinnamon stick, broken in half
½ teaspoon black peppercorns, lightly crushed
¼ teaspoon saffron threads
1½ cups Basmati rice
¾ teaspoon salt
½ teaspoon orange flower water (optional)
2½ cups water
2 tablespoons golden raisins
¼ cup roasted cashews
¼ cup pistachio nuts

heat the ghee or vegetable oil in a wide heavy-bottom saucepan. Stir in the cardamoms, cloves, cinnamon stick, and peppercorns and fry over a gentle heat, stirring constantly, for 2 minutes, until fragrant. Add the saffron threads and Basmati rice to the pan and fry, stirring constantly, for a further minute.

add the salt, orange flower water, if using, and measured water. Stir well to mix. Bring to the boil, then reduce the heat, cover the pan, and cook the rice gently for 15 minutes without removing the lid.

remove the pan from the heat and lightly loosen the rice grains with a fork. (All the water should have been absorbed.) Stir the golden raisins into the rice, cover the pan with a clean dry cloth, and allow the rice to cook in its own heat for a further 5 minutes.

stir both the cashews and pistachios into the rice just before serving. Serve hot.

Serves 4–6
Preparation time: *5 minutes*
Cooking time: *25 minutes*

clipboard: Orange flower water is a delicate flavoring which, although not essential, enhances the subtle flavor of the rice. It is available in many gourmet food stores.

Breads and Accompaniments

Puri Stuffed with Dhal

1 cup dried black beans
4½ cups all-purpose flour
1 fresh green chile, chopped
½ teaspoon salt
vegetable oil for deep frying
fresh cilantro leaves, to garnish

Spices
1 tablespoon aniseed
1 teaspoon coriander seeds
½ teaspoon white cumin seeds
½ teaspoon red chili powder
¼ teaspoon asafetida powder

soak the black beans in water overnight. Rinse them in cold running water and drain well. Sift the flour into a bowl and gradually add enough cold water to make a soft dough. Cover this with a damp cloth and let stand for 30 minutes.

grind the drained beans with the chile, salt, and all the spices to make the stuffing. You can do this in an electric grinder or food processor if wished. Mix well.

divide the dough into 16 portions, using wet hands, and smear each one with a little of the vegetable oil. Flatten each piece of dough and roll out to a 2-inch diameter circle.

wrap a portion of the stuffing in each circle of dough and, with greased hands, roll into smooth balls. Flatten each ball with a rolling pin into a 3-inch round. Heat the oil for deep frying and fry the puri, one at a time, until golden on both sides. Drain on paper towels and serve garnished with cilantro.

Makes 16
Preparation time: *30 minutes*, plus overnight
  soaking time, plus 30 minutes standing time
Cooking time: *20 minutes*

clipboard: Black beans are salted, fermented beans with a salty flavor. They are sold in packs or by weight, and must be soaked for at least 5–10 minutes before use.

Chapatis

2¼ cups whole-wheat flour
1 teaspoon salt
1 cup water
ghee or vegetable oil for greasing
butter, to serve

place the flour and salt in a bowl and make a hollow in the center. Gradually stir in the water, a little at a time, and mix to form a soft, supple dough.

knead the dough on a lightly floured surface for 10 minutes, and then cover the dough and leave in a cool place for 30 minutes. Knead again thoroughly and then divide the dough into 12 equal-sized pieces.

roll out each piece of dough, using a rolling pin on a lightly floured surface, until they form thin round "pancakes."

grease a griddle or heavy-bottom skillet lightly with a little ghee or vegetable oil and place over a moderate heat. Add a chapati to the pan and cook until blisters appear. Press down firmly with a spatula and then turn it over and cook the other side until lightly colored. Remove and keep warm while you cook the other chapatis.

serve brushed with a little butter and folded into quarters.

Makes 12
Preparation time: *15 minutes*, plus
  30 minutes standing time
Cooking time: *12 minutes*

Naan

Naan is a delicious, puffy Indian bread, made with milk and yogurt, which is just right for soaking up spicy curries and baltis. This one is spread with butter and poppy seeds before cooking under a preheated broiler.

3¼ cups all-purpose flour
1½ teaspoons sugar
1 teaspoon salt
½ teaspoon baking soda
½ ounce fresh yeast
⅝ cup warm milk
⅝ cup plain yogurt
ghee or vegetable oil for greasing
½ cup butter
2 tablespoons poppy seeds

sift the flour into a large bowl and stir in the sugar, salt, and baking soda. Dissolve the yeast in the milk and stir in the yogurt. Mix thoroughly with the flour to form a dough.

knead the dough until it is smooth, and then place in a bowl covered with a clean cloth and leave it to rise in a warm place for about 4 hours.

divide the risen dough into 12 equal-sized portions and roll them into balls. On a lightly floured surface, flatten the balls into oblong shapes, using both hands and slapping the naan from one hand to the other.

grease a griddle or heavy-bottom skillet lightly with ghee or vegetable oil and heat it until it is very hot. Cook the naan on one side only, a few at a time. Remove and spread the raw side with butter and poppy seeds. Cook under a preheated hot broiler until browned. Serve hot.

Makes 12
Preparation time: *30 minutes*, plus
 4 hours rising time
Cooking time: *30 minutes*

Paratha

Paratha is a whole-wheat dough, lightly brushed with a little oil or ghee and cooked on a griddle or a heavy-based skillet. It tastes marvellous when served with spicy foods.

2¼ cups whole-wheat flour
1 teaspoon salt
1 cup water (approximately)
4–6 tablespoons melted ghee or 1–1½ tablespoons vegetable oil

place the flour and salt in a bowl. Make a hollow in the center, gradually stir in the water, and work to a soft, supple dough. Knead for 10 minutes, then cover and leave in a cool place for 30 minutes. Knead again very thoroughly, then divide into 6 pieces.

roll out each piece on a floured surface into a thin circle. Brush with melted ghee or vegetable oil and fold in half; brush again, and fold in half again. Roll out again to a circle, about ⅛ inch thick.

grease a griddle or heavy-bottom skillet lightly with a little ghee or vegetable oil and place over a moderate heat. Add a paratha and cook for 1 minute. Lightly brush the top with a little ghee or vegetable oil and turn over. Brush all round the edge with ghee or vegetable oil and cook until golden. Remove from the skillet and keep warm while cooking the rest. Serve hot.

Makes 6
Preparation time: *35 minutes*, plus 30 minutes standing time
Cooking time: *15 minutes*

Puri

Puris are deep fried whole-wheat pancakes, popular in some parts of India. Serve them to accompany spicy sauces and curries, or just as a little snack.

2¼ cups whole-wheat flour, or half whole-wheat and half white all-purpose flour
¼ teaspoon salt
⅝ cup warm water (approximately)
2 teaspoons melted ghee or vegetable oil
oil for deep frying

place the whole-wheat flour and salt in a bowl; sift in the all-purpose flour, if using. Make a hollow in the center, add the warm water gradually, and mix to a dough. Knead in the ghee or vegetable oil, then knead for 10 minutes until smooth and elastic. Cover and set aside for 30 minutes.

divide the dough into 16 pieces. With lightly oiled hands, pat each piece into a ball. Lightly oil a work surface and rolling pin and roll out each ball into a thin circular "pancake."

heat the oil and deep fry the puris very quickly, turning them over once, until deep golden in color. Drain well and serve immediately.

Makes 16
Preparation time: *30 minutes*, plus
30 minutes standing time
Cooking time: *20–30 minutes*

Raita

As popular as chutney, this is a classic Indian accompaniment, consisting of yogurt and cucumber, which helps take some of the heat out of the spicy dishes with which you serve it.

3½ ounces cucumber, thinly sliced, plus extra to garnish
1½ cups plain yogurt
6 scallions, thinly sliced
1 fresh green chile, seeded and finely chopped
cilantro leaves, to garnish
salt

place the cucumber in a colander, sprinkle with salt, and leave to drain for 30 minutes. Dry thoroughly.

mix the yogurt with salt to taste and fold in the cucumber, scallions, and chile. Arrange in a serving dish, garnish with some extra slices of cucumber, and chill until required.

Serves 4
Preparation time: *5 minutes*, plus 30 minutes standing time

clipboard: Raita can also be made using other vegetables as well as cucumber, and with fruit. Banana, for example, makes a particularly good raita.

Cachumber
with onion and tomatoes

This quickly prepared accompaniment is an Indian version of the ever popular tomato salsa. It is delicious as a dip, but also proves an ideal partner to vegetable curries.

1 onion, chopped
1 cup skinned and chopped tomatoes
1–2 fresh green chiles, chopped
1–2 tablespoons vinegar
salt

put the onion, tomatoes, and chiles in a dish. Pour over the vinegar (the mixture must not be too liquid) and salt to taste. Chill before serving.

Serves 4
Preparation time: *5 minutes*

clipboard: A red onion is probably the best variety to use for this spicy onion and tomato dish. Red onions are not so strong as others and are slightly sweet.

Breads

Poppadum

Naan

Parathas

Poppadum
Poppadums are flat, crisp breads with a particularly crunchy texture. They can be either plain or spiced, and in different sizes. They can be served to accompany main meals, or as an appetizer with a sauce or chutneys. They are available in packets in some gourmet food markets and Asian food stores.

Parathas
Breads play a very important part in the Indian diet, and parathas are cooked almost on a daily basis in the great majority of Indian homes. The paratha is a popular flat bread made with whole-wheat flour. Parathas can also be stuffed with various fillings. In Indian cafés, parathas are deep fried and served with freshly barbecued kebobs.

Naan
Naan bread is the exception to most Indian breads in that it is unleavened. It is often used as an accompaniment to curries and baltis—almost as an eating utensil to soak up sauces or pieces of food. Naan are cooked in a tandoor oven, which is heated to a fierce temperature. They are made with yeast and are delicious served hot. Naan can also be flavored with garlic or herbs. The peshawari naan—which comes from Peshawar in Pakistan and is becoming increasingly popular in the West—is stuffed with almonds and is slightly sweet. When it is eaten with a curry, it adds an interesting sweet and sour flavor. Keema naan is stuffed with a filling made of ground meat.

Chapatis

Mini Poppadums

Mini Naan

Chapatis

The chapati is one of the less fattening Indian breads, as it does not contain any fat— though some people in India like to brush it with a little melted butter made from buffaloes' milk, just before serving. It is a flat circular Indian bread, which slightly resembles a pancake, made with whole-wheat flour. Chapatis should be eaten hot out of the pan, when they will be swollen and crisp. If it is not practical to serve it immediately, it can be kept warm by wrapping it in foil. In India, chapatis are cooked over a naked flame so that the bread puffs up. They can also be cooked on a griddle. Chapatis may be filled with chopped spinach flavored with ginger and cumin, in which case they will not be quite as crisp.

Mini Poppadums

Mini-poppadums are now sold in packets in some gourmet and Asian food stores. They are delicious eaten as a snack between meals, or they can be served with chutneys and dips, either as an appetizer or as an accompaniment to a main meal.

Mini Naan

Naan breads come in many shapes and sizes nowadays to suit the particular occasion. Mini-naan are ideal to serve as quick snacks, or they can be served as a first course.

Mango Chutney

Homemade mango chutney is far superior to the commercially prepared varieties. Use firm mangoes, which are just ripe but not yet soft. This chutney will keep for several months in an airtight jar.

2 cups sugar

2½ cups vinegar

2-inch piece of fresh ginger root

4 garlic cloves

2 pounds very firm mangoes, peeled and cut into small pieces

½–1 tablespoon chili powder

1 tablespoon mustard seeds

2 tablespoons salt

⅔ cup raisins or golden raisins

place the sugar and all but 1 tablespoon of the vinegar in a saucepan and simmer for 10 minutes.

blend the ginger, garlic, and remaining vinegar to a paste in a blender or food processor. Add to the pan and cook for 10 minutes, stirring.

add the mango and remaining ingredients to the pan and cook, uncovered, for about 25 minutes, stirring as the chutney thickens. Remove from the heat and allow to cool.

pour into hot sterilized jars, making sure that the lids are airtight.

Makes about 2½ pounds
Preparation time: *35 minutes*
Cooking time: *25 minutes*

Shrimp Relish

This aromatic relish, in which shrimp are spiced with red and green chiles, cumin seeds, turmeric, ginger, and curry leaves, makes a delicious accompaniment to Indian food.

2 tablespoons oil

1 onion, chopped

4 dried red chiles

2 fresh green chiles, chopped

½ teaspoon cumin seeds

½ teaspoon turmeric

1 garlic clove, minced

1-inch piece of fresh ginger root, chopped

4 curry leaves, crumbled

5 ounces shrimp

1 tablespoon vinegar

salt

heat the oil in a pan, add the onion and fry until golden. Crumble in the dried chiles. Add the fresh chiles, cumin seeds, turmeric, garlic, ginger, and curry leaves and fry for 2 minutes. Add the shrimp and cook for 2 minutes.

add the vinegar and season with salt to taste. Simmer, uncovered, for 3–4 minutes, until most of the liquid has evaporated. Serve hot or cold.

Serves 4
Preparation time: *5 minutes*
Cooking time: *20 minutes*

clipboard: Curry leaves are the aromatic leaves of the sweet Nim tree and are available dried. They release a spicy, appetizing smell when they are cooked.

Date and Tomato Chutney

This chutney, which is made with dates, tomatoes, and onions, makes a welcome alternative to the other chutneys that are more usually served with Indian food, such as mango chutney or lime pickle.

8 ounces dates, pitted and chopped
1 x 1-pound can tomatoes
1 onion, chopped
1½-inch piece of fresh ginger root, chopped
1 teaspoon chili powder
1 teaspoon salt
6 tablespoons vinegar

put all the ingredients in a saucepan and stir well. Bring to the boil, then simmer, uncovered, for about 45 minutes, stirring occasionally until thick. Serve cold.

note that extra chili powder and salt may be added if wished, according to taste.

Serves 4–6
Preparation time: *10 minutes*
Cooking time: *45 minutes*

Ginger Chutney

Another unusual chutney, this one is made with fresh ginger root, blended with lemon juice, sugar, golden raisins, and garlic. It does not keep but needs to be eaten fresh.

8 tablespoons lemon juice

2 tablespoons sugar

4 ½ ounces fresh ginger root, finely chopped

½ cup golden raisins

1 garlic clove, minced

salt

place all the ingredients in a blender or food processor and blend to a smooth purée.

transfer the mixture to a small serving dish and chill until ready to serve. Eat within 2 days.

Makes about 1 ¼ cups
Preparation time: *5 minutes*

clipboard: Golden raisins come from grapes that are green when fresh but darken in color when they are dried. In general, lighter-colored golden raisins are obtained by being dried in the shade, while darker ones are obtained by being dried in the sun.

Brinjal Pickle

This pickle is for those who like hot relishes, but the quantity of chiles can be reduced if you prefer a milder taste.

2 pounds eggplants, thinly sliced
1 tablespoon salt
1¼ cups hot water
4 ounces tamarind
2 ounces cumin seeds
1 ounce dried red chiles
2 ounces fresh ginger root, chopped
2 ounces garlic, peeled
1¼ cups vinegar
⅝ cup oil
2 teaspoons mustard seeds
1 cup sugar

sprinkle the eggplants with the salt and leave in a colander for 30 minutes to drain. Pour the hot water on to the tamarind and leave to soak for 20 minutes. Press through a fine strainer and set aside.

put the cumin, chiles, ginger, garlic, and 2 tablespoons of the vinegar into a blender or food processor and blend to a paste.

heat the oil in a large saucepan and fry the mustard seeds until they begin to splutter. Quickly add the spice paste and cook, stirring, for 2 minutes. Add the eggplant, tamarind water, remaining vinegar, and the sugar and stir well. Bring to the boil, then simmer for 30–35 minutes, until the mixture is thick and pulpy.

leave until cold, then pour into sterilized jars and cover with small rounds of waxed paper and seal well. Store in a cool place.

Makes about 3 pounds
Preparation time: *5 minutes*, plus
30 minutes standing time
Cooking time: *40–45 minutes*

Sambal Bajak

A pungent pickle, this is made using onions, garlic, shrimp paste, fresh red chiles, and lime juice. It has a fiery kick, and is not for the faint-hearted!

2 tablespoons oil
3 small onions, finely chopped
4 garlic cloves, finely chopped
1 teaspoon blachan or shrimp paste
4 ounces fresh red chiles, chopped
4 tablespoons lime juice
1 teaspoon salt
1 teaspoon brown sugar

heat the oil in a small skillet, add the onions and garlic, and cook until golden brown. Add the blachan or shrimp paste and fry, stirring and mashing, for 1 minute.

stir in the remaining ingredients and cook, stirring, for 5 minutes, or until the mixture is fairly dry.

allow to cool, then spoon into a jar. Cover and keep refrigerated until required.

Serves 4
Preparation time: *5 minutes*
Cooking time: *15 minutes*

clipboard: Blachan is a strong-smelling, salty shrimp paste, available in cans or packets from specialist food stores. It has a very pungent smell, so you should keep it tightly sealed in the refrigerator once it has been opened. It should always be well fried, or wrapped in foil and roasted, before it is used.

Brinjal Sambal

This eggplant pickle is not excessively spicy, largely because of the addition of coconut milk. It makes a good accompaniment to spicy meat or vegetable dishes.

1 large eggplant
1 small onion, finely chopped
3 fresh green chiles, finely chopped
½-inch piece of fresh ginger root, cut into fine strips
2 tablespoons thick unswetened coconut milk
½ teaspoon salt
4 tablespoons lemon juice

place the eggplant on a cookie sheet and cook in a preheated oven at 350°F for 30 minutes, or until soft. Leave to cool slightly, then slit it open and scoop out the flesh into a bowl.

mash the eggplant flesh with a fork and mix in the remaining ingredients. Taste the Sambal and adjust the seasoning. Serve chilled.

Serves 4
Preparation time: *10 minutes*, plus chilling time
Cooking time: *30 minutes*
Oven temperature: 350°F

Sambal Oelek

with chiles and lemon juice

4 ounces fresh red chiles, chopped
2 tablespoons lemon or lime juice, or vinegar
1 teaspoon sugar
1 teaspoon salt

put all the ingredients into a blender or food processor and blend until the chiles are finely chopped. Adjust the seasoning, to taste. Spoon into a jar, seal with a lid, and keep refrigerated until required.

Serves 4
Preparation time: *5 minutes*

Desserts

Batter Coils in Syrup

1½ cups all-purpose flour
⅓ cup gram or garbanzo bean flour (besan), lightly dry fried
4 tablespoons plain yogurt
¼ ounce fresh yeast
vegetable oil, for deep frying

Syrup
1¼ cups water
1 cup sugar
½ teaspoon ground saffron
½ teaspoon green cardamom seeds, ground

put the all purpose and gram flours in a large bowl and mix in the yogurt, yeast, and enough water to make a thick creamy batter. Set aside for about 2 hours to ferment.

put the water and sugar in a saucepan and stir over a low heat until all the sugar has dissolved. Bring to the boil, still stirring, and cook until the syrup has reached the thread stage (225°F). Just before the syrup is ready, add the ground saffron and ground cardamom seeds.

heat the vegetable oil in a pan until a cube of day-old bread dropped in turns golden in 1 minute. Whisk the batter thoroughly and then pour in a steady stream through a perforated spoon to form coils in the pan below. Make a few coils at a time and deep fry for about 30 seconds, turning them so that they are golden and crisp all over.

remove the coils from the pan and drain on paper towels. Immerse them in the prepared syrup for 3–4 minutes to soak up as much syrup as possible. Remove the coils and serve immediately while they are hot and crisp.

Serves 4–6
Preparation time: *15 minutes*, plus
2 hours standing time
Cooking time: *20 minutes*

Coconut Dessert

There is nothing like the flavor of fresh coconut. The preparation for this dish is a little complicated, but it's well worth the effort.

2 fresh coconuts
2 cups boiling water
1 cup sugar
1¼ cups rice flour
2 eggs, beaten
⅓ cup slivered almonds
shredded coconut, to decorate

make some holes in the "eyes" of the coconuts and then carefully drain out the liquid over a bowl and set aside for later.

crack open the coconuts and separate the flesh from the shells. Grate the flesh into a bowl and then pour the boiling water over it. Let stand for 15 minutes and then strain the liquid through a strainer lined with double cheesecloth, held over a bowl.

gather up the cheesecloth and squeeze out as much coconut milk as possible. Discard the coconut in the cloth. Mix the strained coconut milk with the liquid extracted from the coconuts and then beat in all the remaining ingredients.

pour the mixture into a large heavy-based saucepan and bring to the boil. Reduce the heat and simmer until the liquid thickens, stirring constantly. Pour into a greased 8-inch round baking pan and bake in a preheated oven at 350°F for 30 minutes, until browned. Serve hot, decorated with coconut.

Serves 4
Preparation time: *35 minutes*, plus
  standing time
Cooking time: *30 minutes*
Oven temperature: 350°F

Mango Ice Cream

2 cups canned mango pulp
3 tablespoons liquid honey
2½ cups heavy cream
⅓ cup ground almonds
4 egg whites
mint leaves, to decorate

warm the mango pulp in a saucepan over a gentle heat and then stir in the honey until melted. Remove from the heat and stir in the cream and the ground almonds until they are evenly mixed. Set aside and cool.

pour the mango ice cream mixture into a freezer container and place in the freezer. Freeze for about 4 hours, or until the mango mixture is just beginning to freeze around the edges and becoming slushy.

remove the container from the freezer and turn out the mango ice cream into a bowl. Carefully break up the mixture with a fork.

beat the egg whites in a clean bowl until stiff and then gently fold them into the half-frozen mixture. Return to the freezer container and freeze for a further 4 hours, until solid. Remove the ice cream from the freezer about 20 minutes before serving to soften slightly. Decorate with mint leaves.

Serves 8
Preparation time: *20 minutes*
Freezing time: *8 hours*

Deep Fried Milk Pastries

4½ cups milk
8 tablespoons lemon juice
⅔ cup semolina
vegetable oil for deep frying

Syrup
1¼ cups water
5 cardamoms
5 cloves
1 cup sugar
2 teaspoons rosewater

heat the milk in a saucepan, add the lemon juice, and bring to the boil. Don't worry when it curdles. Boil for 5–10 minutes and then leave to cool. Drain off the whey (the thin watery part of the milk), leaving the curds (thicker parts of the milk) behind. Tie the curds up in a double thickness of cheesecloth and place in a strainer. Weight down and leave overnight.

mix the resulting cheese (panir) with the semolina on the following day, to form a dough. Break into about 15 equal-sized pieces and roll into smooth balls. Heat the oil for deep frying until a ball of dough, when dropped into the pan, immediately starts to sizzle and floats to the surface.

deep fry the balls in batches until evenly golden brown. Remove with a slotted spoon and drain on paper towels. Keep them warm in a low oven while you make the syrup.

bring the water to the boil in a pan with the cardamoms and cloves. Reduce the heat, add the sugar, and stir until dissolved. Increase the heat and boil rapidly, without stirring, until the syrup starts to thicken. Cool slightly and add the rosewater. Serve the pastries warm in the syrup.

Serves 4–6
Preparation time: *30 minutes*, plus
  overnight standing time
Cooking time: *25 minutes*

Kheer

This Indian variation on rice pudding, delicately flavored with golden raisins and slivered almonds or pistachios, is absolutely wonderful.

⅓ cup long-grain rice
7½ cups milk
⅓ cup golden raisins (optional)
sugar to taste
⅝ cup light cream

To decorate
slivered almonds
rose petals

put the rice and 4½ cups of the milk in a heavy-bottom pan. Cook gently at simmering point for 45–60 minutes, until most of the milk has been absorbed.

add the remaining milk and the golden raisins, if using. Stir well and simmer until thickened. Remove from the heat and add sugar to taste.

leave until completely cold, stirring occasionally to prevent a skin forming, then stir in the cream.

turn into small dishes and serve cold, sprinkled with slivered almonds or pistachios. Decorate with rose petals.

Serves 4
Preparation time: *5 minutes*, plus
 chilling time
Cooking time: *1–1¼ hours*

Almond Barfi

The Indians are good at imaginative milk desserts, and this one is no exception. The milk is slowly cooked until it becomes thick and lumpy, when it is flavored with almonds and crushed cardamoms.

3 cups full-cream milk
¼ cup sugar
⅓ cup ground almonds
6 cardamoms, peeled and crushed

cook the milk in a large heavy-bottom saucepan for about 1¼ hours, until it is reduced to a thick lumpy consistency. Stir occasionally and be careful not to let the milk burn.

stir in the sugar, then add the almonds and cook for 2 minutes. Pour into a buttered tray and sprinkle with the crushed cardamoms. Serve warm, cut into squares.

Serves 4
Preparation time: *5 minutes*
Cooking time: *1¼ hours*

Shrikand

This yogurt-based dessert looks as good as it tastes. Flavored with saffron and rosewater, it is guaranteed to impress your guests.

4 cups plain yogurt
¼ teaspoon saffron threads
2 tablespoons sugar
1 tablespoon rosewater

To decorate
1–2 teaspoons cardamom seeds, crushed
1 tablespoon pistachio nuts, shelled and chopped

turn the yogurt into a strainer lined with some cheesecloth and leave it to drip over a bowl for 6 hours. Put the dried curds—there will be about 10 ounces—into a bowl and beat in the saffron. Add the sugar and taste; add a little more if you like, but it should not be too sweet.

mix in the rosewater, a little at a time, until the mixture resembles thick cream. Cover and chill until required.

spoon into individual bowls and decorate with the cardamoms and pistachios to serve.

Serves 4
Preparation time: *5 minutes*, plus 6 hours
standing time, plus chilling time

clipboard: Rosewater is used to flavor creams, ice creams, and pastries, as well as liqueurs and wines. It is available from some good gourmet food markets.

Mawa

The ingredients are very simple, the preparation is simpler still, but something magical happens during the cooking time to turn this into a magical Indian-style candy.

7½ cups full-cream milk
3–4 tablespoons sugar
2 leaves varq (silver leaf)
handful of edible flowers (e.g. nasturtiums
or pansies), to decorate

cook the milk in a large heavy-bottom saucepan for about 1¼ hours, until it is reduced to a thick, lumpy consistency. Stir occasionally and be careful not to let the milk burn.

add the sugar and continue cooking for 10 minutes.

spread the mixture on a lightly buttered plate: it should be a light cream-colored, softly set candy.

cut into wedges and serve cold decorated with strips of varq and edible flower petals.

Serves 4–6
Preparation time: *5 minutes*
Cooking time: *1 hour 25 minutes*

Carrot Halva

Carrots rarely feature on the dessert menu, but this recipe is set to change all that and carrots take a well-deserved bow, with the help of a little corn syrup and golden raisins.

5 cups milk
8 ounces carrot, finely grated
6 tablespoons butter
1 tablespoon light corn syrup
½ cup sugar
⅓ cup golden raisins or raisins

To decorate
1 teaspoon cardamoms
2 leaves varq (silver leaf)

place the milk and grated carrot in a heavy-bottom saucepan and cook over a high heat, stirring occasionally, until the liquid has evaporated. Add the butter, syrup, sugar, and golden sultanas or raisins. Stir until the butter and sugar have melted, then cook for 15–20 minutes, stirring frequently, until the mixture starts to leave the side of the pan.

pour into a shallow buttered dish and spread evenly. Decorate with cardamoms and strips of varq. Cut into slices and serve warm or cold.

Serves 4–6
Preparation time: *5 minutes*
Cooking time: *45–50 minutes*

Kulfi

Blanched almonds combine with milk, heavy cream, and rosewater to produce this unusual and impressive ice cream. Garnished with rose petals, it looks marvellous.

1½ cups blanched almonds
7½ cups milk
1 cup sugar
1¼ cups heavy cream
2 tablespoons rosewater

place the almonds in a bowl, cover with cold water, and set aside. Reserve 1¼ cups of the milk and bring the rest to the boil in a large heavy-bottom or nonstick saucepan. Simmer until the milk is reduced by half, stirring from time to time to insure that any skin or solids that cling to the side of the pan are well mixed in.

drain the almonds and place three-quarters of them in a blender or food processor with the reserved milk. Blend the mixture for a few seconds until the almonds are coarsely ground; the mixture should be crunchy. Add the almond mixture and sugar to the hot milk and continue simmering for a further 10–20 minutes, stirring constantly. Remove the pan from the heat and let cool to room temperature, then place in the refrigerator until well chilled.

chop the remaining almonds coarsely and add them to the chilled milk along with the heavy cream and rosewater, stirring thoroughly, so that the ingredients are well mixed. Pour into molds—cone-shaped metal molds are traditional—and freeze until solid. Transfer to the refrigerator 20 minutes before serving, then unmold, and serve.

Serves 8
Preparation time: *1 hour*, plus freezing time
Cooking time: *40 minutes*

Index

A

amchoor, 97
accompaniments
  brinjal pickle, 223
  brinjal sambal, 226
  cachumber, 211
  date and tomato chutney, 218
  ginger chutney, 220
  mango chutney, 214
  shrimp relish, 216
  raita, 208
  sambal bajak with chiles and
    lemon juice, 224
  sambal oelek, 228
almonds
  almond barfi, 242
  chicken biriyani, 64
  kulfi, 250
  lamb with almonds, 98
  rice with vegetables, 182
  roast chicken with almonds, 74
  roghan ghosht, 102
  vegetable biriyani, 188
aloo
  aloo cakes, 134
  aloo sag, 166
  tamatar aloo, 168
amotik, 56
anglerfish
  amotik, 56
  fish and coconut soup, 16
  fish kebobs, 46
aniseed, 10, 46
asafetida, 10
asafetida powder, 144

B

Baked spiced fish, 54
baltis
  balti beef and broccoli with onion
    and chopped tomatoes, 138
  balti chicken with green bell
    pepper, 92
  balti lamb Madras with tomatoes
    and coconut flakes, 112

balti mixed vegetables, 177
banana, raita, 208
Bangalore chicken curry, 90
barbecues
  barbecued king shrimp, 50
  chicken tikka masala, 81
Basmati rice, 9, 131
  chicken pilau, 76
  kitcheree, 186
  pilau rice, 194
  rice with vegetables, 182
  saffron rice, 180
  shrimp pilau, 58
  shrimp and spinach rice, 192
batters
  batter coils in syrup, 232
  fish fritters, 60
  pakora, 32
  puri, 206
  spiced fried shrimp, 28
  vegetable rolls with quick
    chutney, 152
bay leaves, 158
bean sprouts, spiced chicken soup, 18
beans
  balti mixed vegetables, 177
  black 198
  gram and bean dhal with marrow
    and chile, 162
  sprouting mung dhal with fennel
    seeds and ginger, 165
beef
  aloo and potato cakes, 134
  balti beef and broccoli with
    onion and chopped tomatoes,
    138
  beef buffad, 126
  Calcutta beef curry, 122
  chile fry with pepper and
    tomatoes, 132
  ground meat samosas, 24
  kofta in yogurt, 136
  meatball curry, 120
  spicy beef in yogurt, 124
  stuffed bell peppers with beef,
    rice, and tomatoes, 129
Bengal cooking, 7
besan, *see* gram flour

bharta, 170
bhuna ghosht with coriander and
  lemon, 116
Bihar cooking, 7
biriyani
  chicken biriyani, 64
  vegetable biriyani, 188
blachan, 224
black beans, 198
  puri stuffed with dhal, 198
black mustard, 115
black onion seeds, 10
Bombay cooking, 7
bowls, 13, 104
breads, 212-3
  chapatis, 200, 213
  naan, 202, 212
  pappadoms, 212
  paratha, 204, 212
brinjal pickle, 223
brinjal sambal, 226
broccoli, balti beef and broccoli
  with onion and chopped
  tomatoes, 138
brown Basmati rice, 131
brown mustard, 115
buffad, beef buffad, 126
buffaloes' milk, 22
butter, 6, 9, 22

C

Cabbage, fried chile cabbage
  with potatoes, peas, and
  carrots, 142
cachumber, 211
Calcutta beef curry, 122
cardamom, 10, 81
cardamom pods, 184
carrots
  balti mixed vegetables, 177
  carrot halva, 248
  fried chile cabbage with potatoes,
    peas, and carrots, 142
  vegetable biriyani, 188
cashews
  chicken biriyani, 64

shrimp pilau, 58
  vegetable biriyani, 188
cauliflower
  balti mixed vegetables, 177
  cauliflower curry, 144
  phul gobi with multicolored bell
    peppers, 156
  vegetable biriyani, 188
cayenne pepper, 138
chapatis, 200, 213
charcoal-grilled fish, 43
cheese
  cream cheese kofta curry, 150
  panir mattar, 160
  vegetable biriyani, 188
chicken
  balti with green bell pepper, 92
  Bangalore chicken curry, 90
  chicken biriyani, 64
  chicken korma, 66
  chicken and lentils with spinach
    and tomatoes, 72
  chicken makhani, 88
  chicken molee with ginger and
    creamed coconut, 86
  chicken pilau, 76
  chicken stock, 11
  chicken tikka, 78
  chicken tikka masala, 81
  chicken vindaloo, 70
  Kashmiri chicken, 82
  palak murg, 84
  roast chicken with almonds, 74
  spiced chicken soup, 18
  tandoori chicken, 69
chiles, 6, 10, 158, 159, 184-5
  Bangalore chicken curry, 90
  chile fry with bell pepper and
    tomatoes, 132
  ekuri, 30
  fried chile cabbage with potatoes,
    peas, and carrots, 142
  gram and bean dhal with marrow
    and chilli, 162
  phul gobi with multicolored bell
    peppers, 156
  shrimp relish, 216
  preparation, 30

sambal bajak, 224
sambal oelek with chiles and
    lemon juice, 228
vegetable curry, 174
chili powder, 138, 185
chopping boards, 13
chopping knives, 13
chutneys
    date and tomato chutney, 218
    ginger chutney, 220
    mango chutney, 214
    quick chutney, 152
cilantro, 32, 116, 159, 170
    bangalore chicken curry, 90
    bhuna ghosht, 116
    kofta in yogurt, 136
cilantro leaves, preparation, 136
cinnamon, 10, 86, 185
clarified butter, 6, 9, 22
cloves, 10, 108
coconut, 6, 158
    chicken molee, 86
    coconut pudding, 234
    cream cheese kofta curry, 150
    fish and coconut soup, 16
    spicy steamed mussels with
        coconut and yogurt, 53
coconut flakes, balti lamb Madras
    with tomatoes and, 112
coconut milk, 6, 10, 38, 126
    brinjal sambal, 226
    fish in coconut milk, 38
    fish and coconut soup, 16
coconut oil, 9
cod
    baked spiced fish, 54
    curried fish balls, 40
    fish fritters, 60
colanders, 13
coriander seeds, 10, 116, 184
cottonseed oil, 9
cream cheese kofta curry, 150
creamed coconut, 126
    chicken molee with ginger and
        creamed cocnut, 86
cucumber, raita, 208
cumin, 10, 48
cumin seeds, 130, 142, 185

curd cheese
    cream cheese kofta curry, 150
    panir mattar, 160
    vegetable biriyani, 188
curries, 6, 7-8
    Bangalore chicken curry, 90
    Calcutta beef curry, 122
    cauliflower curry, 144
    chicken korma 66
    chicken vindaloo, 70
    cream cheese kofta curry, 150
    curried fish balls, 40
    meatball curry, 120
    pork vindaloo, 115
    shrimp curry with onion and
        garlic, 48
    spicy okra, 154
    vegetable curry, 174
curry leaves, 159, 216
curry powder, 7-8

Date and tomato chutney, 218
deep fried milk pastries, 239
desserts
    almond barfi, 242
    batter coils in syrup, 232
    carrot halva, 248
    coconut pudding, 234
    deep fried milk pastries, 239
    kheer, 240
    kulfi, 250
    mango ice cream, 236
    mawa, 246
    shrikand, 244
dhals
    gram and bean dhal with squash
        and chile, 162
    masoor, 131
    masoor dhal, 191
    moong dhal, 131
    puri stuffed with dhal, 198
    sprouting mung dhal with fennel
        seeds and ginger, 165
dhana jeera, 90
dhansak, lamb dhansak, 110

doughs
    batter coils in syrup, 232
    chapatis, 200
    ground meat samosas, 24
    naan, 202
    paratha, 204
    puri, 206
    puri stuffed with dhal, 198
dried red chiles, 184-5

Eastern Indian cooking, 7
eggs
    ekuri, 30
    shrimp pilau, 58
eggplants, 158
    bharta, 170
    brinjal pickle, 223
    brinjal sambal, 226
    stuffed eggplants, 148
    vegetable curry, 174
ekuri, 30
equipment, 10, 13, 104-5

Fats, 9
fennel, 76
fennel seeds, 10
    sprouting mung dhal with fennel
        seeds and ginger, 165
fenugreek, 10
fish, 7
    amotik, 56
    baked spiced fish, 54
    charcoal-grilled fish, 43
    curried fish balls, 40
    fish in coconut milk, 38
    fish and coconut soup, 16
    fish fritters, 60
    fish kebobs, 46
    fish stock, 11
    fish tandoori, 44
fish slices, 105
flour, 60, 130

freezing, stocks, 10
fried chile cabbage with potatoes,
    peas, and carrots, 142
fritters
    fish fritters, 60
    spiced fried shrimp, 28
fruit, raita, 208
fruits, 158-9

Garam masala, 112
garbanzo beans, 40, 97, 130, 172
    garbanzo bean flour, 60
    gram and bean dhal with squash
        and chile, 162
    kabli channa, 172
    lamb dhansak, 110
garlic, 92, 159
ghee, 6, 9, 22
ghosht
    bhuna ghosht with coriander and
        lemon, 116
    rogan ghosht, 102
ginger, 54, 84, 158
    chicken molee, 86
    ginger chutney, 220
    root preparation, 132
    sprouting mung dhal with fennel
        seeds and, 165
Goan cooking, 7
golden raisins, 220
    ginger chutney, 220
    pilau rice, 194
    shrimp pilau, 58
    rice with vegetables, 182
    vegetable biriyani, 188
grains, 130-1
gram and bean dhal with squash
    and chile, 162
gram flour, 32, 40, 60
grams see also garbanzo beans;
    lentils, 172
graters, 13
green chiles, Bangalore chicken
    curry, 90
green bell peppers, balti chicken

with, 92
ground beef, aloo, and potato
    cakes, 134
ground lamb
    kheema do pyaza, 100
    lamb kebobs, 97
ground meat samosas, 24

H

Haddock
    curried fish balls, 40
    fish kebobs, 46
halibut
    charcoal-grilled fish, 43
    fish and coconut soup, 16
    fish kebobs, 46
    fish tandoori, 44
halva, carrot halva, 248
herbs, 158-9
Hindu cooking, 6, 7, 8

I

Ice cream, mango ice cream, 236
Indian split pea soup, 20

K

Kabli channa, 172
Kashmiri chicken, 82
Kashmiri cooking, 6
kebobs
    fish kebobs, 46
    lamb kebobs, 97
    prawn kebobs, 34
kheema do pyaza, 100
kheer 240
kitcheree, 186
knives, 13
kofta
    cream cheese kofta curry, 150
    kofta in yogurt, 136
korma
    chicken korma, 66

lamb korma, 106
kulfi, 250

L

Ladies fingers, 159
    spicy okra, 154
ladles, 104
lamb
    balti lamb Madras with tomatoes
        and coconut flakes, 112
    kheema do pyaza, 100
    lamb with almonds, 98
    lamb dhansak, 110
    lamb kebobs, 97
    lamb korma, 106
    raan, 108
    roghan ghosht, 102
    stuffed bell peppers with rice and
        tomatoes, 129
lemon, bhuna ghosht with
    coriander and, 116
lemon juice, sambal oelek with
    chiles and lemon juice, 228
lentils, 32, 172, 191
    chicken and lentils with spinach
        and tomatoes, 72
    kabli channa, 172
    kitcheree, 186
    lamb dhansak, 110
    masoor dhal, 131, 191
lime juice, sambal bajak, 224
lovage, 148

M

Macademia nuts, 18
mango, 158
    mango chutney, 214
    mango ice cream, 236
    mango powder, 97
marinades
    barbecued jumbo shrimp, 50
    chicken korma, 66
    chicken makhani, 88
    chicken tikka, 78
    fish tandoori, 44

raan, 108
    shrimp kebobs, 34
    spiced fried shrimp, 28
    tandoori chicken, 69
masala, 43
    charcoal-grilled fish, 43
    chicken tikka masala, 81
    garam masala, 112
    lamb with almonds, 98
    lamb dhansak, 110
masoor dhal, 131, 191
mawa 246
measuring jugs, 104
meat, 6, 7
    ground meat samosas, 24
    kofta in yogurt, 136
meat see also beef; lamb; pork
meatballs
    kofta in yogurt, 136
    meatball curry, 120
milk
    almond barfi, 242
    Calcutta beef curry, 122
    carrot halva, 248
    deep fried milk pastries, 239
    kheer, 240
    kulfi, 250
    mawa, 246
    naan, 202
mini-naans, 213
mini-pappadoms, 213
mint, 159
mint leaves, roghan ghosht, 102
mixing bowls, 13
moong dhal, 131
    chicken and lentils with spinach
        and tomatoes, 72
    kitcheree, 186
Mughal cooking, 6, 7
mung beans, 130, 165
    sprouting mung dhal with fennel
        seeds and ginger, 165
mussels, spicy steamed mussels
    with coconut and yogurt, 53
mustard oil, 6, 7, 9
mustards, 10, 115

N

Naan, 202, 212
Northern Indian cooking, 6
nutmeg, 10
nuts
    chicken biriyani, 64
    pilau rice, 194
    vegetable biriyani, 188

O

Oils, 9
okra, 154, 159
    spicy okra, 154
    vegetable biriyani, 188
onions
    cachumber, 211
    pakora, 32
orange flower water 194

P

Pacific shrimp, 34
pakora, 32
palak murg, 84
pancakes, puri, 206
panir, 160
    cream cheese kofta curry, 150
    panir mattar, 160
    vegetable biriyani, 188
pans, 105
pappadoms, 212
paprika, 82
paratha, 204, 212
paring knives, 13
Parsee dishes, lamb dhansak, 110
parsley, 32
pastes, chicken biriyani, 64
pastries
    deep fried milk pastries, 239
Patna rice, 9
    saffron rice, 180
peas
    balti mixed vegetables, 177
    fried chile cabbage with potatoes,
        peas, and carrots, 142

ground meat samosas, 24
Indian split pea soup, 20
panir mattar, 160
spiced pea soup, 22
vegetable biriyani, 188
vegetable curry, 174
vegetable samosas, 27
peppers
    balti chicken with green bell
        pepper, 92
    chile fry with bell pepper and
        tomatoes, 132
    phul gobi with multicolored bell
        peppers, 156
    stuffed bell peppers with beef,
        rice, and tomatoes, 129
pestle and mortar, 13
phul gobi with multicolored bell
        peppers, 156
pickles
    brinjal pickle, 223
    brinjal sambal, 226
    sambal bajak, 224
pilau
    chicken pilau, 76
    pilau rice, 194
    shrimp pilau, 58
pineapple, shrimp pilau, 58
pistachios, vegetable biriyani, 188
pork
    bhuna ghosht with coriander and
        lemon, 116
    pork vindaloo, 115
potatoes
    aloo cakes, 134
    aloo sag, 166
    balti mixed vegetables, 177
    cream cheese kofta curry, 150
    fried chile cabbage with potatoes,
        peas, and carrots, 142
    pakora, 32
    tamatar aloo, 168
    vegetable curry, 174
    vegetable rolls with quick
        chutney, 152
    vegetable samosas, 27
Punjabi cooking, 6
puri, 206

puri stuffed with dhal, 198

Quick chutney, vegetable
    rolls with, 152

Raan, 108
raisins
    aloo and potato cakes, 134
    roast chicken with almonds, 74
raita, 208
red chiles, 158, 159, 184-5
red lentils, masoor dhal, 131
red onions, 211
relishes, shrimp relish, 216
rice, 6, 9, 130-1
    brown Basmati, 131
    chicken biriyani, 64
    chicken pilau, 76
    kheer, 240
    kitcheree, 186
    pilau rice, 194
    rice with vegetables, 182
    saffron rice, 180
    shrimp pilau, 58
    shrimp and spinach rice, 192
    stuffed bell peppers with beef,
        rice, and tomatoes, 129
    white Basmati, 131
roast chicken with almonds, 74
roghan ghosht, 102
rosewater, 244

Saffron, 10, 64
saffron rice, 180
saffron threads, 184
sambal
    brinjal sambal, 226
    sambal bajak, 224
    sambal oelek with chiles and

lemon juice, 228
samosas
    ground meat samosas, 24
    vegetable samosas, 27
sauces
    chicken makhani, 88
    chicken tikka masala, 81
    curried fish balls, 40
    fish in coconut milk, 38
scrambled eggs, ekuri, 30
sesame oil, 9
shrikand, 244
shrimp
    barbecued jumbo shrimp, 50
    shrimp curry with onion and
        garlic, 48
    shrimp kebobs, 34
    shrimp pilau, 58
    shrimp relish, 216
    shrimp and spinach rice, 192
    spiced chicken soup, 18
    spiced fried shrimp, 28
shrimp paste, sambal bajak, 224
silver leaf, 180
skillets, 105
skimmers, 105
sole, fish in coconut milk, 38
soups
    fish and coconut soup, 16
    Indian split pea soup, 20
    spiced chicken soup, 18
    spiced pea soup, 22
Southern Indian cooking, 6
spiced chicken soup, 18
spiced fish, baked, 54
spiced fried shrimp, 28
spiced pea soup, 22
spices, 7, 184-5
    biriyani spices, 64
    cauliflower curry spices, 144
    lamb dhansak, 110
    preparation, 8
    puri stuffed with dhal, 198
    selection, 10
spicy beef in yogurt, 124
spicy okra, 154
spicy steamed mussels with coconut
    and yogurt, 53

spinach
    aloo sag, 166
    chicken and lentils with spinach
        and tomatoes, 72
    pakora, 32
    palak murg, 84
    shrimp and spinach rice, 192
    spinach with tomatoes, 147
split peas, Indian split pea soup, 20
sprouted mung beans, 130
sprouting mung dhal with fennel
        seeds and ginger, 165
stocks, preparation, 10-11
stuffed eggplants, 148
stuffed bell peppers with beef, rice,
        and tomatoes, 129
swedes, balti mixed vegetables, 177
syrup
    batter coils in syrup, 232
    deepfried milk pastries, 239

Tamarind, 6, 7, 56
amotik, 56
tamatar aloo, 168
tandoori
    fish tandoori, 44
    tandoori chicken, 69
tikka
    chicken tikka, 78
    chicken tikka masala, 81
tomatoes
    balti beef and broccoli with onion
        and chopped tomatoes, 138
    balti lamb Madras with tomatoes
        and coconut flakes, 112
    cachumber, 211
    chicken and lentils with spinach
        and tomatoes, 72
    chicken makhani, 88
    chilli fry with pepper and
        tomatoes, 132
    cream cheese kofta curry, 150
    date and tomato chutney, 218
    fried chile cabbage with potatoes,
        peas, and carrots, 142

kheema do pyaza, 100
lamb with almonds, 98
preparation, 150
spicy okra, 154
spinach with tomatoes, 147
stuffed bell peppers with beef,
    rice, and tomatoes, 129
tamatar aloo, 168
vegetable curry, 174
turmeric, 10, 34, 168, 185
turners, 105
turning bowls, 104

U

Utensils, 10, 13, 104-5

V

Varak, 180
vegetable oil, 9

vegetables, 158-9
    balti mixed vegetables, 177
    rice with vegetables, 182
    vegetable biriyani, 188
    vegetable curry, 174
    vegetable rolls with quick
        chutney, 152
    vegetable samosas, 27
    vegetable stock, 11
vindaloos
    chicken vindaloo, 70
    pork vindaloo, 115

W

Western Indian cooking, 7
white Basmati rice, 131
white cumin seeds, 142
whole-wheat flour, 130

Y

Yogurt, 10, 98
cauliflower curry, 144
chicken korma, 66
chicken tikka, 78
cream cheese kofta curry, 150
Kashmiri chicken, 82
kheema do pyaza, 100
kofta in yogurt, 136
lamb korma, 106
naan, 202
raan, 108
raita, 208
roast chicken with almonds, 74
roghan ghosht, 102
shrikand, 244
spicy steamed mussels with
    coconut and yogurt, 53
spicy beef in yogurt, 124

Z

Zucchini
    rice with vegetables, 182
    vegetable biriyani, 188

Acknowledgments

Photo Credit
Jean Cazals: front cover
Graham Kirk: back cover

Special photography by Graham Kirk

All other photos:
Octopus Publishing Group / Jean Cazals, Jeremy Hopley, Graham Kirk,
James Murphy, Peter Myers.

Home economist
Sunil Vijayakar